The Music Producer's Guide to Distortion

Published by Stereo Output Limited, company number 11174059.

ISBN number 978-1-739996-55-0

The Music Producer's Guide is an independent series of books, and has not been authorised, sponsored, or otherwise approved by Ableton AG or any other company where screenshots of their products appear herein.

Please go to www.stereooutput.com to contact us or follow us on various social media channels.

Stereo Output

Introduction

Distortion is the alteration of the shape of an information-bearing signal. In music, this signal is an audio wave.

If you have any experience of music production, you've experienced distortion. It is the fuzz that occurs when you push a mixer channel's amplitude too high, or when the master output of a plugin is set too loud. It is often represented on audio equipment as a red line, and as producers, we are trained to avoid "going into the red", especially when producing using a computer.

Whilst unintentional distortion is usually undesirable, many producers use distortion intentionally to improve their productions. In lesser amounts, it gives a sound warmth and body. In substantial amounts, it makes sounds crackle and screech. It is so prevalent in contemporary music production that you may not notice its presence when used subtly.

It is an effect that is harnessed both by producers in studios and by music listeners who appreciate the distortion inherent in vinyl or good-quality amplifiers and speakers.

Understanding how distortion works and using distortion in your music production are vital skills.

From electric guitars and synthesizers to vocals, distortion is on almost every instrument and voice in popular music. Besides adding character and flavour to the sound, distortion can help producers achieve certain effects in their music, such as adding colour or emphasis to certain elements of a track.

In this book, I will provide you with a succinct but comprehensive guide to distortion and how it works in music production.

By the end of this book, you will understand what distortion is, the history and context of its use, and how to use contemporary distortion techniques to improve your music production.

There are some key technical terms used in this book, many of which you may already be familiar with from your music production experience. These are highlighted in **bold** and are summarised in a glossary in the back of this book.

There are also references to specific parameters within plugins. When I refer to a plugin parameter, I do so in *italics*.

Before we begin our journey into distortion, we must start with a primer on the very phenomenon that underpins all music: harmonics.

Chapter 1: Harmonics

Consonance and dissonance.

These are the building blocks of musical harmony. Two consonant frequencies, played together, sound pleasant. Two dissonant frequencies, played together, sound unpleasant. This is because of the **harmonic series**.

The harmonic series defines the mathematical relationship between different musical notes. Its discovery allowed people to understand why certain combinations of notes sounded pleasant together, and to create new combinations that sounded good.

Pythagoras is credited with the contemporary discovery of harmonics using an instrument called a monochord.

A monochord was like a single guitar string – a string held at tension, with two fixed points. A moveable bridge served as the fret, as illustrated in Figure 1.1.

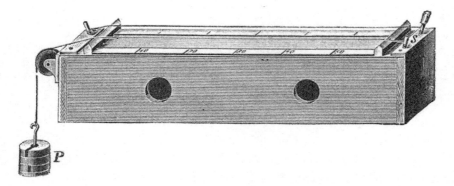

Figure 1.1: A monochord (image from Bibliothek allgemeinen und praktischen Wissens für Militäranwärter Band III, 1905).

With the bridge set to one side, plucking the string of the monochord generated a frequency. Pythagoras discovered that moving the bridge to precise mathematical ratios of this frequency generated consonant notes. These ratios are shown in Figure 1.2:

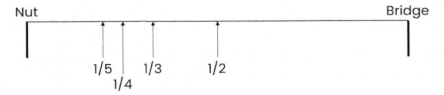

Figure 1.2: Precise mathematical ratios on a monochord.

The consonant notes generated by these ratios are crucial to our present-day music.

For example, imagine that the note of this monochord, when the bridge is not in use, to be C. Using the bridge to divide the string according to precise mathematical ratios (in this case 1/5, 1/4, 1/3 and 1/2) generates the notes of the musical scale, as shown in Figure 1.3:

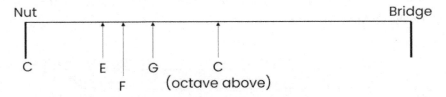

Figure 1.3: Precise mathematical ratios on a monochord converted to note values.

The discovery of the mathematical relationships between different notes aided the discovery of why certain combinations of notes sound pleasant together. This is because of the mysterious human preference for musical harmony – humans prefer notes with a simple mathematical ratio governing their relationship. This is the phenomenon that underpins most musical scales.

The harmonic series does not stop at the relationship between notes, however – it also applies to single notes. When a musical instrument, such as a monochord, piano, or guitar, is played, a vibration is created at the frequency of the note played. This is called the fundamental frequency. Besides this fundamental, there is a vibration at double the fundamental frequency, triple the fundamental frequency, four times the fundamental frequency, and so on. These are harmonic **overtones**, often termed as '**harmonics**. This is illustrated in Figure 1.4:

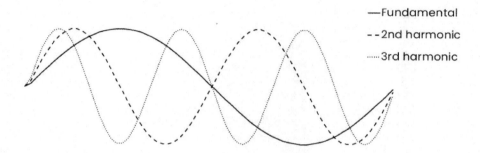

—Fundamental
- -2nd harmonic
······3rd harmonic

Figure 1.4: The harmonic series.

For example, if a guitar string is plucked at 440Hz, you will hear harmonics. Table 1.1 shows the first seven:

Table 1.1: The first seven harmonics of 440Hz.

Harmonic	Pitch	Nearest musical note
Fundamental	440Hz	A4
Second harmonic	880Hz	A5
Third harmonic	1320Hz	E6
Fourth harmonic	1760Hz	A6
Fifth harmonic	2200Hz	C#
Sixth harmonic	2640Hz	E7

Seventh harmonic	3080Hz	G7

Each of these harmonics is usually a lower amplitude than the harmonic below it, although the extent to which they are lower depends on the instrument played. An example of such a harmonic series is shown in Figure 1.5:

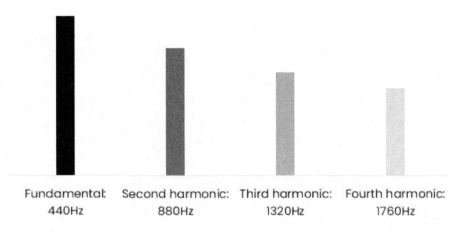

| Fundamental: | Second harmonic: | Third harmonic: | Fourth harmonic: |
| 440Hz | 880Hz | 1320Hz | 1760Hz |

Figure 1.5: Harmonics descend in amplitude as you move up the harmonic series.

Our ears cannot pick out these individual harmonics; we perceive each note as the fundamental frequency. The harmonics add colour to the tone.

This psychoacoustic effect is so powerful, in fact, that where the fundamental is absent from a note, but its harmonics are present, the listener still perceives the fundamental as being there. This phenomenon is known as the **missing fundamental**.

The extent and amplitude of harmonics allow us to perceive the timbre of a sound. Harmonics allow us to recognise people by their voices, locate sounds and distinguish musical instruments from one another.

A great starting point for studying harmonics is a subtractive synthesizer. This is because the harmonics it generates are precise, repeatable and controllable (unlike non-electronic musical instruments, which are usually complex and difficult to control). In synthesizers, devices called oscillators create various waveforms. These waveforms create different combinations of harmonics. For example, a sawtooth wave generates each harmonic of the fundamental, as shown in Figure 1.6. This gives it a warm, rich timbre:

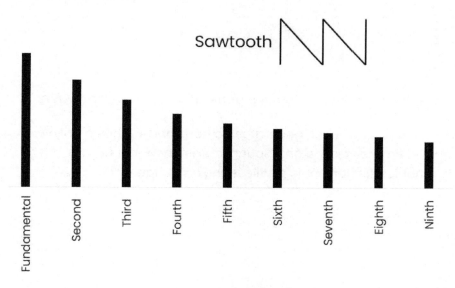

Figure 1.6: The harmonics generated by a sawtooth wave.

Unlike a sawtooth wave, a square wave only generates odd harmonics of the fundamental, as seen in Figure 1.7. This gives it a glassy, metallic timbre:

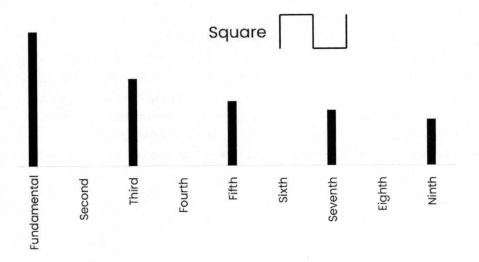

Figure 1.7: The harmonics generated by a square wave.

A sine wave, however, generates no harmonics. It has a hollow, muted timbre. It is the only sound in existence that has no harmonics. Its harmonic profile is shown in Figure 1.8:

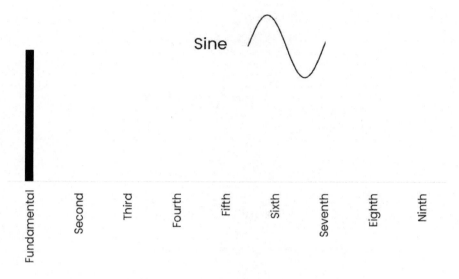

Sine

Fundamental Second Third Fourth Fifth Sixth Seventh Eighth Ninth

Figure 1.8: The harmonics generated by a sine wave.

The timbre of these waveforms is all different – a sawtooth wave sounds warm and rich, a square wave sounds glassy and bright, and a sine wave sounds hollow and thin.

You can view these harmonics for yourself in your DAW software using a spectrum analyser – you can usually do this by adding the spectrum analyser plugin as an effect to the same channel as the instrument, after the instrument and effects plugins.

A spectrum analyser provides a moving visualisation of the amplitude of each frequency, using an algorithm called Fast Fourier Transform, which transforms the sound of your instrument into a readable graph.

These visualisations are quite intuitive once you become familiar with them. The frequency is represented along the x-axis (from left to right), and the amplitude is represented on the y-axis (from bottom to top). Thus, the amplitude at each frequency is represented, as shown in Figure 1.9:

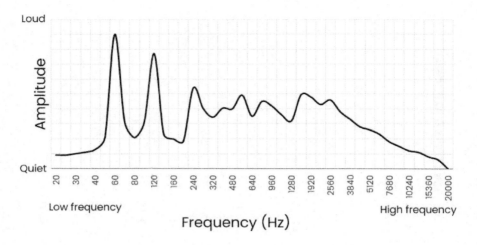

Figure 1.9: An example spectrum analysis.

Look at Figure 1.10 below. Notice the fundamental frequency, its harmonics, and how the harmonic peaks correspond to a mathematical multiple of the fundamental:

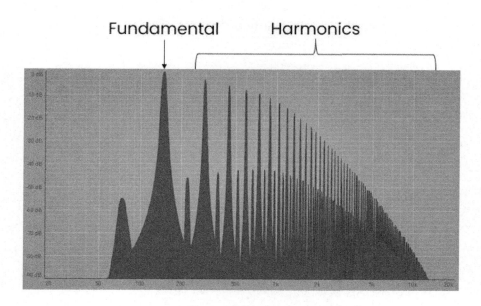

Figure 1.10: *Harmonics on a spectrum analyser.*

If you are interested in learning more about harmonics, I suggest you recreate this in your own DAW. Load a subtractive synthesizer plugin, switch all the filters off, and play each waveform on a single oscillator: a square, followed by a sawtooth, followed by a sine wave. Consider the individual qualities of each waveform. Does one sound smoother than the other? Warmer than the other? Brighter than the other?

This is subjective, but you may find that the harmonics generated by the sawtooth wave are warmer and more inviting than the harmonics generated by the square wave. The mathematical difference between the two is key – the square wave contains odd harmonics alone. Remember this for later.

You should also load some other instruments and look at the spectrum analysis of them – you will find some are more balanced than others, some have louder harmonics than others, and some are more harmonically stable than others. It's incredible to discover that the huge variety of timbres in existence come from subtle harmonic changes.

Distortion generates harmonics, too. For example, compare the two spectrum analyses in Figure 1.11. One is a piano note on its own. The other is the same piano note, highly distorted.

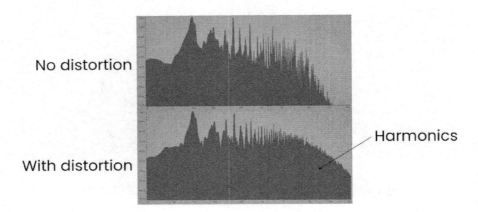

No distortion

With distortion

Harmonics

Figure 1.11: A spectrum analysis of a piano without distortion and with distortion.

As you can see, the distortion has generated a great deal of harmonics, particularly in the higher frequency range. This has significantly changed the timbre of the sound, making it harsher and brasher.

Now that we've considered the harmonic series, and its importance for our perception of timbre, let's look at how analogue distortion occurs.

Summary

- When a note is played, it generates a fundamental frequency, which is usually the frequency of the note played. It also generates harmonics.

- Harmonics are overtones that accompany the fundamental frequency. Us humans find these harmonics to be pleasing.
- Harmonics are multiples of the fundamental frequency. In isolation, they form a musical scale.
- The balance of these harmonics affects our perception of a sound's timbre.

Chapter 2: How Analogue Distortion Occurs

In today's environment, we're used to using computers, which transmit information perfectly. If you email a document you're working on to a friend, the document they receive will be an exact copy of the document you sent.

The analogue world, however, audio transmission is an imperfect process. All analogue devices modify the signal through the addition of distortion. Some devices add more distortion than others, and the timbre of the distortion added depends on the individual device. The outcome of this distortion is the addition of harmonics to the signal, changing the timbre of the sound.

The history of distortion is intertwined with the history of recorded music. From the earliest days of using electronics to record music, distortion occurred at any point when a tape recorder or a vinyl record was pushed near its amplitude limit. In this chapter, we shall examine individual analogue distortive processes.

Before we start, it's worth considering a common terminological question: what is the difference between **distortion, saturation,** and any other term commonly found, such as **overdrive**?

Essentially, think of it as a spectrum. Distortion is commonly considered the buzziest, most harsh effect (think of a distorted electric guitar), saturation means to subtly warm up a sound (think of when you receive a track back from a mastering engineer), and overdrive sits somewhere in the middle between the two (think of when you add a bit of *Overdrive* in a synthesizer plugin).

However, all three are derived from the processes set out in this chapter, and so, for our purposes, the differences between the terms are irrelevant. Scientifically, it's all distortion. So don't worry – in this book, the terms can be used interchangeably. My intention in writing this book is for you to understand the fundamental process, as opposed to awkward, ambiguous terms.

With that said, let's begin our journey into the world of distortion by examining the workings of tube amplifiers.

Tubes

In the days of analogue technology being the dominant form of sound recording and reproduction, one major distortive process was the use of amplifiers, particularly guitar amplifiers. Their role was to transform the tiny vibrations of guitar strings into loud notes. These devices used vacuum tube amplification. Some vacuum tubes are shown in Figure 1.12:

Figure 1.12: Vacuum tubes. Image courtesy of Stefan Riepl (Quark48) / CC BY-SA 2.0 DE

These glass vacuum tubes controlled an electrical current by creating a vacuum around a pair of electrodes. These tubes inherently added a small amount of natural distortion through their usual operation. When any signal exceeded the capacity of the tube, however, they added a great deal of natural harmonics.

Guitar players noticed that if they were to turn their amplifiers up to an excessive point, their guitars would sound messier, fuzzier, and dirtier. Whilst many sound engineers initially considered this an undesirable artefact, guitar players began to experiment and fall in love with this sound. Tube amplification is still in use to this day – usually on high-end devices, given its prohibitive cost.

The tube, also known as a valve in British English, amplifies sound by harnessing the phenomenon of thermionic emission. A heated filament, known as a cathode, emits electrons. These electrons are attracted by the plate. The plate is an anode, which is an electrode that attracts electrons when a positive charge is applied. By placing these two components, the cathode and the plate, together inside a vacuum, the electrons flow freely from one end of the device to the other, because there is no air resistance.

A simplified diagram of such a tube is shown in Figure 1.13:

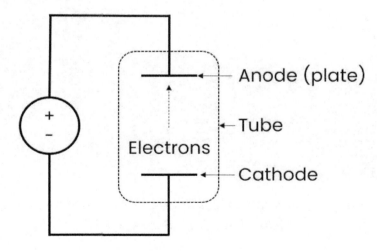

Figure 1.13: A diagram of a vacuum tube.

If one adds a charged grid of fine wire between the cathode and the anode, its voltage can control the flow of these electrons. A more negative voltage repels the electrons back towards the cathode so that fewer get through to the anode. A more positive voltage allows more electrons through. When in the presence of a fluctuating signal, such as an audio signal, these fluctuations occur quickly. Thus, the small voltage changes in the guitar signal are amplified into large current changes on the anode.

The transmission of audio information through a tube is imperfect, i.e., the audio sent into the tube is not the same as the audio coming out. The more this circuit is pushed to its limits, the more harmonics are added – these harmonics are caused by distortion of the audio wave. Tube amplifiers add second and third harmonics in particular.

The second harmonic is one octave above the note itself, and whilst it often isn't particularly audible, it adds body and presence. The third harmonic, meanwhile, forms a musical 12th harmonic, i.e., an octave plus a fifth above the fundamental, which softens the tone.

The quirks of tubes add a great deal of natural character – the higher the intensity of the input signal, the more distorted the tone. This happens on a curve, so the amount of distortion increases rapidly as the tube reaches its saturation point. This creates a natural way for a guitarist using a tube amplifier to add emphasis, without increasing the overall intensity of the tube amp's output.

This nonlinear relationship is displayed in Figure 1.14 – notice how once this amplifier reaches its saturation point, the relationship between input level and output level decouples –the higher the input level is pushed, the greater the divergence between the input and output level. The greater the divergence, the greater the distortion.

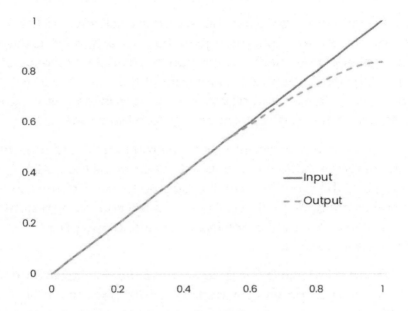

Figure 1.14: As the increasing input amplitude begins to saturate the tube, the relationship between input and output amplitude begins to diverge.

Tape

Tape was once the main method of recording music. It has mostly been replaced by computers, but is still in use in many studios to add warmth and distortion to a sound. In this section, we shall explore how it does this.

Figure 1.15: A tape recorder.

Tape machines store their tape on two reels. During recording and playback, the tape is passed from one reel to another. Between these reels are two heads: the recording head and the playback head. The function of the recording head is to record incoming audio onto the tape, and the function of the playback head is to play this audio back. There is also sometimes an erase head, which erases the audio signal from the tape.

The tape is a plastic film with a surface made of iron oxide powder. As the tape moves past the recording head, the powder is magnetised in a way that keeps the recording of the audio signal.

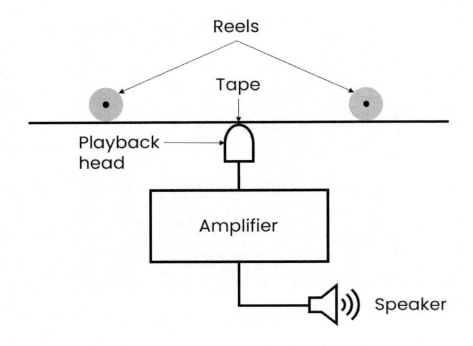

Figure 1.16: A diagram of a tape recorder.

When the audio input voltage exceeds a certain threshold, the iron oxide molecules of the tape reach their maximum magnetic potential and cannot be polarised any further. The signal becomes compressed and distorted, as the tape cannot accurately record the frequencies or amplitude of the original signal. This adds pleasing harmonics and creates a warmer sound, at a cost of losing high-end clarity.

One of the main variables of tape recording is the speed at which the tape moves through the tape path and across the heads. This is measured in inches per second, shortened to **IPS**. Common settings are 7.5, 15 and 30 IPS The faster the tape speed, the better the reproduction of higher frequencies, as more information can be encoded, with 7.5 IPS considered 'lo-fi'.

In addition, tape recorders use a feature called **bias**. This is an ultrasonic signal introduced into the recording to help maximise its fidelity, particularly at higher frequencies. Incorrect biasing adds some degradation to the sound.

A significant factor in tape recording is **tape hiss**. Tape always has some natural low-level hiss because of the size of the magnetic particles used to make the tape. This hiss is particularly audible if lower quality tape is used, or the recording amplitude is too low.

Tapes are also subject to artefacts caused by the tape recorder's mechanism. One such artefact is called **Wow**, which is subtle frequency modulation caused by slight changes in the speed of the motors. Another is called **Flutter,** which is subtle frequency change caused by the tape's movements as it is drawn across the playback head.

To conclude, tapes are capable of several forms of distortion:

1. Saturation caused by exceeding the magnetic capacity of the tape. This adds pleasing, warm sounding harmonics at a cost of losing some high frequencies.
2. Loss of high frequency content caused by a slower tape recording speed.
3. Degradation caused by incorrect biasing.
4. Hiss naturally present on the tape, which can be quite significant at lower volumes.
5. Wow and flutter caused by aberrations in the machine's motors.

Transistors

In the mid-20th century, manufacturers began using transistors in electronic circuits. These were used as an alternative to tubes in amplifiers, being cheaper and less fragile. When pushed to their limits, transistors distorted, but often the distortion was harsher and less warm sounding than their tube counterparts. Transistor distortion contained a lot of odd harmonics, as opposed to the even harmonics of tubes.

During the 1970s, designers began experimenting with a concept called **bias**.

Amplifier components have a **bias point**, which defines where the crossover point of a sound wave is. This is shown in Figure 1.17:

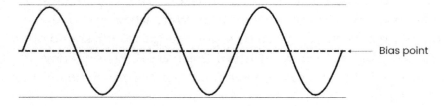

Figure 1.17: The bias point of an amplifier.

However, if the bias point is too low, the troughs of the waveform will breach the capacity and lead to distortion. This can generate crunchier, harder distortion, as seen in Figure 1.18:

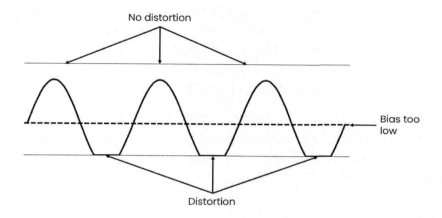

Figure 1.18: Moving the bias too low generates distortion on one side of the waveform.

Equally, if the bias is too high, the peaks of the waveform will breach the capacity and lead to warm, smooth distortion, as shown in Figure 1.19:

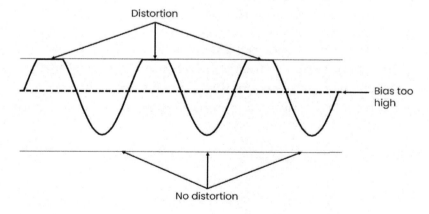

Figure 1.19: Moving the bias too high generates distortion on the other side of the waveform.

This quirk of electronics gave amplifier designers of the period a great deal of freedom to experiment with different ways of creating bias and distortion to achieve the optimal sound from their transistor amplifiers. Instead of the default, cold, transistor sound, producers could use transistors to generate 'warm' distortion. For example, a high bias point came to be known for its 'bluesy' sound. This type of clipping, with its off-centre bias point, was known as **asymmetrical clipping**.

Amplifiers also harnessed more traditional clipping distortion, known as **symmetrical clipping**, where the bias point was at the centre, with both sides of the waveform being clipped to the same degree, as seen in Figure 1.20:

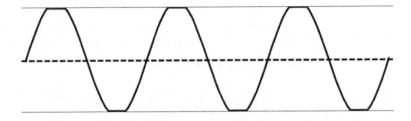

Figure 1.20: Symmetric clipping is where both sides of the waveform are clipped.

Now, let's look at the science behind symmetrical clipping. As you can see in the figure above, the clipping makes the waveform 'squarer'. If you were to compare the harmonics of a sine wave before and after this clipping occurred, they would look like Figure 1.21:

Before

Fundamental   Second harmonic   Third harmonic   Fourth harmonic   Fifth harmonic

After

Fundamental   Second harmonic   Third harmonic   Fourth harmonic   Fifth harmonic

Figure 1.21: Distortion has added harmonics to this sine wave.

As you can see, this distortion has added a third and fifth harmonic where previously there was none.

If you cast your memory back to the section on harmony, you will recall that square waves in synthesis produce odd harmonics only. This is the same set of harmonics created by symmetrical clipping. This also means that after symmetrical clipping, the harmonics take on a similar character to those of a synthesized square wave – characterful, but cold and hollow.

In summary, amplifiers provide the widest range of distortion. Whilst the distortion inherent in traditional analogue amplifiers is minimal and warming, the distortion inherent in amplifiers designed to distort is huge, ranging from mild 'warming' to destruction.

This can occur through two main routes: clipping and biasing.

In the next section, we shall explore another common way that distortion can occur: compression.

Compression

Compression is the process of automatically attenuating peaks in gain. Essentially, when a compressor detects an audio signal has breached a set threshold, it attenuates the level of that signal according to a fixed ratio. Compression is such an important topic, in fact, that I've written a whole book about it, called *The Music Producer's Guide To Compression*, which is available on Amazon and at many other online bookshops.

Let's have a look, in Figure 1.22, at the spectrum analysis of a single sine wave at roughly 100Hz:

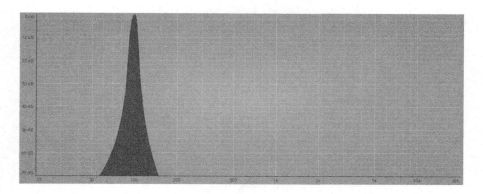

Figure 1.22: The spectrum analysis of a sine wave at 100Hz.

As we can see, there's a single frequency spike. This is what we'd expect from a sine wave because a sine wave contains no harmonics. However, if we add some compression to the sine wave, some harmonics appear, as shown in Figure 1.23:

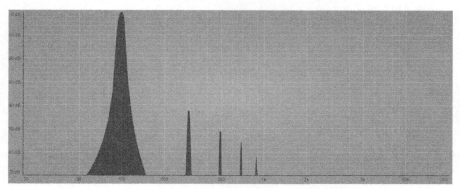

Figure 1.23: Compression has added harmonics to this sine wave.

Why could this be?

The reason is that the compressors do not work statically – they are always attenuating the gain (attacking) or reducing the attenuation (releasing). This quick oscillation changes the waveform of the signal.

We can see this on an oscilloscope. Compare the two waves of Figure 1.24, and you'll see a very slight squaring of the peaks of the sine wave, generating odd harmonics:

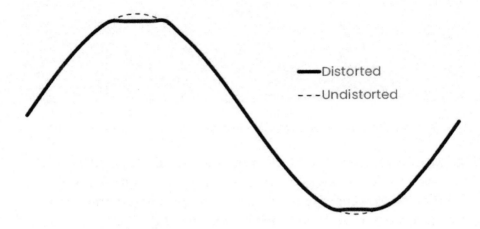

Distorted

- - - Undistorted

Figure 1.24: Look at the very slight flattening of the peak in the distorted wave.

Now we know that compression adds a small amount of harmonic distortion, we must also consider the additional layer of complexity added by vintage-simulating compressors, which simulate valves or tubes.

Often, this means that the distortion naturally added through compression will be besides the type of distortion employed by the plugin. For example, a plugin that aims to emulate tube compression will not only add harmonics through its compression process, but will add further harmonics through its tube simulation process. An example of this is Klanghelm's wonderful *MJUC jr.* plugin, which adds a far higher degree of harmonics than Ableton Live's standard compressor.

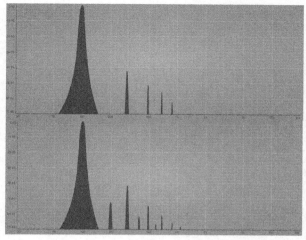

Ableton Live's compressor

MJUCjr compressor

Figure 1.25: Tube compressors, or digital compressors designed to emulate them, add additional harmonics.

As you can see from Figure 1.25, the odd harmonics are louder when using the tube compression plugin than when using Ableton's digital compression plugin. You will also see, however, that a few even harmonics have also been added to the signal – this helps contribute to the feeling of 'warmth' added by the compressor. This is why it can sometimes feel like adding a compressor has 'warmed up' a track.

On this basis, when producing music, assign your devices based on your goals – if you want to warm up a sound, but you do not wish to control its dynamics with any great amount of precision, is compression the most appropriate tool for the job?

In the next section, we'll explore another common form of distortion: vinyl distortion.

Vinyl

Vinyl, just like tape, is an inherently distortive medium of recording.

Vinyl records have a groove imprinted as a spiral into the record. Within these grooves are the analogue waveforms of the sound, as seen in Figure 1.26:

Figure 1.26: Vinyl grooves.

A motor rotates the vinyl record at a certain speed, typically 33, 45 or 78 revolutions per minute (RPM). A **tonearm**, with a **stylus** connected, picks up these grooves. This is shown in Figure 1.27:

Figure 1.27: A stylus playing a record.

The stylus is a small crystal of diamond or sapphire mounted at the very end of a lightweight metal needle. As this crystal vibrates, these microscopic bounces are transmitted up the needle to an electromagnetic device containing a piezoelectric crystal. This crystal generates an electrical signal that is fed to the amplifier, converting the microscopic grooves on the vinyl record into an audible sound.

This analogue mechanical process leads to some distortive processes:

1. Vinyl adds some harmonic distortion because of the limitations of perfectly capturing a waveform in a physical medium. This process adds a small amount of both odd and even harmonics, which are often considered the most pleasing.
2. Tracks destined for vinyl must be mastered using specific techniques. To prevent high frequency signals like hi-hats from becoming overly sibilant during playback, some high frequency content is removed – more than would be removed for a digital master. This adds to a feeling of 'warmth'.

3. The tiny grooves in vinyl records pick up particles of dust. This is heard on the record as a distinctive **'crackle'** and is particularly audible between tracks. Crackle can also be caused by inferior-quality vinyl material that was manufactured with impurities.
4. Records can wear down over time, particularly with repeated plays. This tends to affect the details of high frequencies first.
5. As the record goes on and the needle approaches the centre of the record, additional distortion can occur. This is because there is more vinyl groove per second available at the longer grooves at the start of the record than the shorter grooves at the end. The wavelengths, therefore, become shorter and harder for the stylus to track accurately.

It would be reasonable to assume that these distortive limitations would make vinyl an undesirable format – however, sales have proven that it is highly resilient. Even after digital file storage made both CD and cassette tape redundant formats for home listening, vinyl sales underwent a resurgence. Whether this is due to the vinyl sound, the physicality of the format or because it is fashionable is up for debate – however, the vinyl sound has stood the test of time.

In summary, vinyl distortion is known for a slight 'warming' of a sound, with a slight increase of harmonics and a slight reduction in sibilant frequencies. Next, let's look at how filters can generate distortion.

Filters

Most synthesizers have a filter. A filter shapes the sound of a synthesizer by allowing the user to select which frequencies can pass through.

Some synthesizers, as part of the filter, include a **Drive** function.

Filter Drive is a general term used to describe a variety of distinct types of distortion. It can mean distorting the signal before the filter, distorting the output of the filter, adding distortion to a feedback loop within the filter, and so on. Regardless of the underlying technique, *Filter Drive* creates a warm, gentle distortion.

It's rare for analogue, hardware synthesizers to have a specific, controllable *Filter Drive* parameter. Often, this distortion is built into the synthesizer's circuitry and is enjoyed as part of the synthesizer's sound, such as on the Minimoog or Korg MS20.

However, *Filter Drive* is often added to software synthesizers as a controllable parameter. In these cases, *Filter Drive* describes some attempt by the filter designer to replicate some type of analogue filter distortion. An example of such a filter, in Lennar Digital's Sylenth1, is in Figure 1.28:

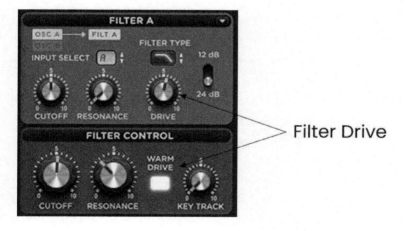

Figure 1.28: The Filter Drive parameter.

Because there are a variety of techniques that can underpin *Filter Drive*, it is not feasible to summarise the function with a precise distortion technique – however, in music production, it is an important type of distortion, as software designers will endeavour to emulate warm, well-known distortive filters.

Should your synthesizer sound be a crucial element of your track, using *Filter Drive* may be highly desirable, because the distortion will probably interact beautifully with the filter itself. This is particularly the case on higher-end synthesizers such as Xfer's *Serum*.

Now that we have considered analogue distortion, let's analyse forms of distortion that exist only in the digital realm.

Summary

- Analogue devices add distortion to a signal.
- This distortion manifests as harmonics being added to the signal.
- Analogue distortion tends to be considered 'warm' sounding.

Chapter 3: The Digital Realm

In the previous section, we looked at analogue distortion. Much of this is because of clipping; distortion that stems mostly from analogue circuits being forced to exceed their capacity. Analogue audio exists in the physical space, with audio waves represented using voltage fluctuations. The real world can be thought of as analogue.

However, most audio production nowadays takes place on a computer. Computers work in discrete digital values, representing audio in bits and bytes of code. Whereas analogue audio has an infinite number of values, digital has a limited number of values, constrained by the properties of computer audio files.

As an analogy, think of a clock. Whilst the real passage of time is analogue and infinite, we represent time in seconds, which are discrete values.

This gives rise to two possibilities for distortion:

1. Distortion effects that exploit the conversion of analogue audio to digitally encoded audio. This is known as **bitcrushing**.

2. Distortion effects that seek to emulate the distortive properties of analogue audio using code. This covers a variety of techniques, particularly **waveshaping**.

Let's explore these two possibilities.

Computer storage uses a unit called a **bit**, which can be set to two values: 0 or 1. All computing is built from combinations of these bits.

This means that, to store audio on a computer, analogue signals must be converted into digital bits.

If we wish to convert an analogue passage of audio, we must do two things:

1. Take measurements of the audio at regular intervals.
2. Store each of these snapshots using bits.

This leads to two considerations:

1. How often do we wish to capture these measurements of audio?
2. How detailed do we want each measurement to be?

There is a delicate balance to be struck. If we capture too few measurements, and they're not detailed enough, the resulting file won't sound like a good representation of the original. If we capture too many snapshots and there's too much detail, the computer files will be big and computationally expensive.

This gives rise to two terms: the **sample rate** and the **bit depth**. The sample rate governs how many snapshots (called samples) that are taken per second, and the bit depth governs how detailed each sample is.

For example, look at this audio wave in Figure 3.1:

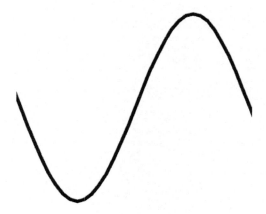

Figure 3.1: A simple, unsuspecting audio wave.

You can see that it's reasonably smooth-looking. Now let's convert it to digital – in this case, stored over 8 bits and 8 samples. First, let's superimpose the sample rate and bit depth, as shown in Figure 3.2:

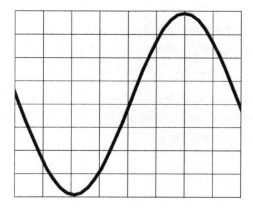

Figure 3.2: The simple, unsuspecting audio wave with a sample rate and bit depth superimposed.

Now, let's convert the waveform to digital by constraining it to the grid, as shown in Figure 3.3:

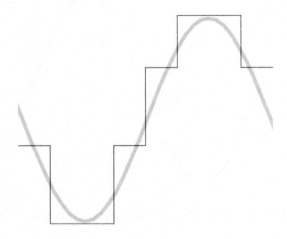

Figure 3.3: The simple, unsuspecting audio wave has been converted into a digital audio wave that bears little resemblance to the original.

You can see that the smooth curves of the waveform have become jagged edges, and therefore will be a poor approximation of the original when played back.

If we expand the grid to 16 frames and 16 bits, we can see in Figure 3.4 that the resemblance to the original improves slightly. This will sound closer to the real thing:

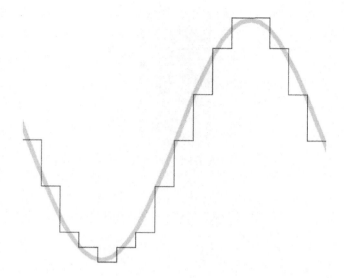

Figure 3.4: By increasing the bit size and sample rate, a more accurate rendition of the audio wave can be created.

Default computer audio uses a 44.1kHz sample rate at a depth of 16 bits. A 44.1kHz sample rate means 44,100 measurements of audio per second. Bit depth is expressed as powers of 2, so 16-bit audio implies that each of the 44,100 'snapshots' per second have 65,536 bits of information. This means, after some additional processing, a very accurate representation of the original sound wave.

Ordinarily, when recording audio, a more accurate depiction of the sound wave is better. However, some producers have found that degrading the bit depth, sample rate, or both, creates digital distortion effects, adding a distinctive hiss or crunch to the sound.

To intentionally reduce the sample rate of a piece of audio is known as **downsampling**, and to reduce the bit rate (i.e., bit reduction) is known as **bitcrushing**.

Most plugins do both, as shown in Figure 3.5:

Figure 3.5: Ableton Live's Redux plugin.

Bitcrushing and downsampling plugins offer a powerful variety of creative effects, such as:

- Many different combinations of degrees of bitcrushing and downsampling.
- Additional effects such as filters or traditional saturation.
- An **LFO** (Low Frequency Oscillator) to vary distortion over time This will make the parameters of the distortion change cyclically.

This makes these digital effects useful to the creative producer, as the distortion can be anything from slight warming to destruction.

Whilst bitcrushing often adds odd-order harmonics, just like many other forms of distortion, downsampling is a more brutal form of distortion, adding non-harmonic frequencies, which form a digital 'fuzz'. We shall explore these later in the book.

For now, let's explore another method of digital distortion: waveshaping.

In the last chapter, we considered how analogue devices distort sound. However, nowadays, a lot of distortion in music-making occurs in the digital DAW realm. Whether this is a fat-sounding virtual synthesizer that emulates an analogue counterpart, or a plugin to emulate a vintage compressor, this distortion mimics analogue distortion to create a warm sound.

In any effects device, something must happen to a signal between the plugin's input and output (otherwise it wouldn't be an effects device!). This is where one of the most important aspects of digital distortion comes in: *waveshaping*.

Waveshaping is an umbrella term for several techniques where the waveform of the sound undergoes a transformation of its timbre or dynamics, but with no significant changes to the frequency. In distortion, this involves the addition of harmonics.

To begin this process, visualise an audio wave. If we wished to reference specific points on that audio wave, we could do so numerically. The centre point of the wave would be 0, its highest point would be 1, and its lowest point would be -1. This is shown in Figure 3.6:

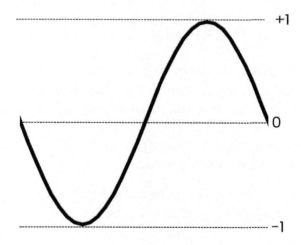

Figure 3.6: A way to mathematically represent points on an audio wave.

We could then program a **transfer function**, which would tell the computer how to alter that wave. For example, we could tell it that when the input audio wave is at -0.5, it should output -0.3. Or we could tell it that when the input audio wave is at -1, it should output 1. This way, we could automatically alter the shape of the wave as it works its way through our system. This process is waveshaping.

The easiest way to visualise waveshaping is on a graph, as shown in Figure 3.7:

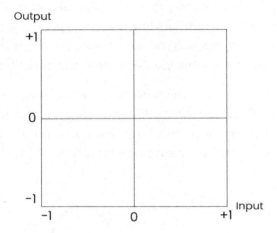

Figure 3.7: A graph showing these mathematical points across two axes – one representing the input amplitude, and the other representing the output amplitude.

The input waveform goes from left to right, and the output waveform goes from bottom to top.

For example, look at this waveshaper in Figure 3.8 – this waveshaper does nothing to the signal:

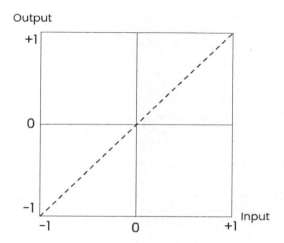

Figure 3.8: A waveshaper that outputs the same signal that you input into it.

If you look along the input axis, you'll see that where there's a -1 input signal, the output signal is also -1. Where the input signal is +0.5, the output signal is also +0.5.

However, this next waveshaper in Figure 3.9 would invert the signal, i.e., turn it upside down:

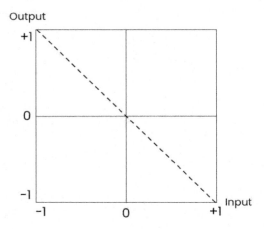

Figure 3.9: A waveshaper that inverts the input.

As you can see, an input value of −1 gives you an output value of +1. An input value of +0.5 gives you an output signal of −0.5. To help you visualise this, I've illustrated these two points in Figure 3.10:

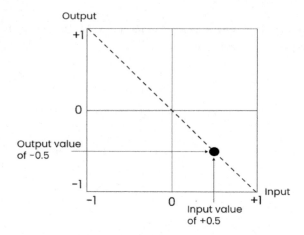

Figure 3.10: A further explanation of the waveshaper that inverts the input.

Now that we understand the basics of waveshaping, we can look at more interesting uses for it.

For example, what would happen if we used this waveshaper in Figure 3.11?

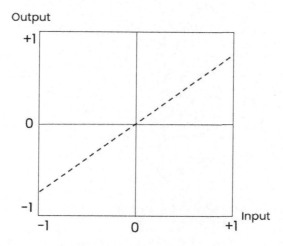

Figure 3.11: An example waveshaper.

As you can see, an input value of -1 creates a -0.8 output. An input value of +1 creates a +0.8 output. This means that the waveshaper reduces the peak level of the wave. Let's have a look in Figure 3.12 at what would happen if we put a sine wave through this waveshaper:

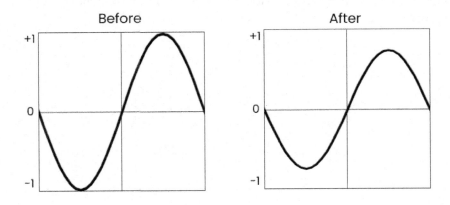

Figure 3.12: A sine wave before and after the waveshaper.

As we can see, the waveshaper has reduced the amplitude of the sound wave.

We can now begin considering ways to use the waveshaper to create harmonics. For example, you'll recall that a square wave contains odd harmonics only. How would we use a waveshaper to convert a sine wave into a square wave?

It's simple – we set up a waveshaper so that if the input signal isn't at point 0, the waveshaper pushes it to either –1 or +1, as shown in Figure 3.13:

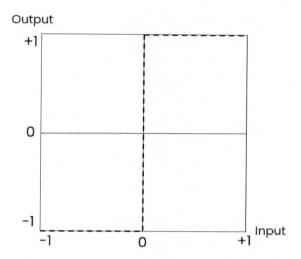

Figure 3.13: A waveshaper that converts every part of the input to either -1 or +1.

This means that the sine wave is converted into a square wave, as shown in Figure 3.14:

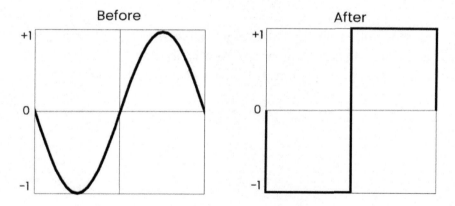

Figure 3.14: A sine wave before and after entering a waveshaper that converts it to a square wave.

Unfortunately, this makes for a boring effects device – after all, who wants to convert everything into a square wave? Fortunately, the addition of odd harmonics while maintaining the original timbre of the sound isn't too difficult; all the waveshaper must do is allow some values of the waveform to behave naturally, thus maintaining some of the instrument's timbre. An example of a waveshaper that does this is shown in Figure 3.15:

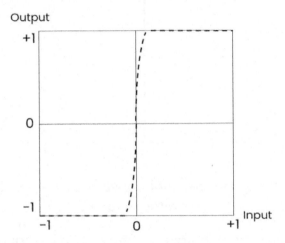

Figure 3.15: This waveshaper allows some of the wave's natural shape to remain.

As you can see in Figure 3.16, this gentler waveshaper has allowed some of the sine wave's shape to remain in place, creating something between a triangle wave and a square wave:

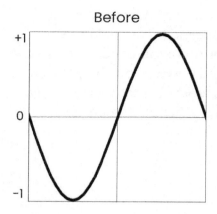
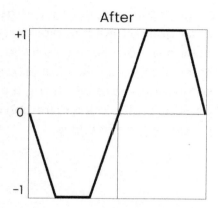

Before

After

Figure 3.16: In this waveshaper, some of the sine wave's natural shape is preserved.

Smooth-shaped transfer functions add more subtle harmonics to a waveform, whereas sharp-shaped transfer functions are far richer in harmonic content.

Waveshaping is one of many techniques that plugin modellers use to create realistic emulations of analogue distortion. However, there are some plugins that bring the waveshaping process to the surface, allowing you to create and change a waveshape.

Should you wish to explore waveshapers further, I highly recommend that you download a waveshaper for yourself and try it. An example is AudioThing's *Wave Box*, which, as of writing, has a free demo available for download on AudioThing's website. What you'll find is that you can achieve some interesting results quickly, but that simple unprocessed waveshaping can sometimes sound cold and digital.

What this means for you as a producer is that the world of distortion plugins operates on simple principles. However, the development of these plugins into something that imbues your music with warmth and feeling is an incredible skill.

Many producers who have larger budgets prefer the sound of analogue distortion to digital; the peculiarities of analogue equipment are often said to add warm, character harmonics. To some extent, I agree – but on a limited budget, you can achieve some fantastic results using digital plugins. In fact, there are many analogue-emulating distortion devices that contemporary producers use and love.

Chapter 4: A Discussion of Contemporary Distortion

In this chapter, we will take a step away from the technical elements of distorting sounds and look at distortion from an artistic perspective.

We know from experience that we have our own preferences with distortion. For example, you may find Primal Scream's highly distorted track *Accelerator* highly unpleasant, pedestrian, or simply perfect. Everyone's tastes are different. Whereas most people will agree that a track washed out with reverb sounds like a mess, or a track with no bass lacks energy, distortion is a highly subjective effect, which depends upon the listener's own taste.

On this basis, we need to consider the amount of distortion used in a track within the context of the intended audience. Broadly, a completely clean, undistorted sound will often sound cold. However, it's very rare to hear a track produced in a completely 'clean' manner, as even compression during the mastering process adds distortion. Most music listeners enjoy a 'sweet spot', where the distortion isn't made intentionally clear, but adds warm, pleasing harmonics. Many listeners also enjoy more extreme distortion, which can add a harsh, fuzzy veneer to the sound. This is illustrated in Figure 4.1:

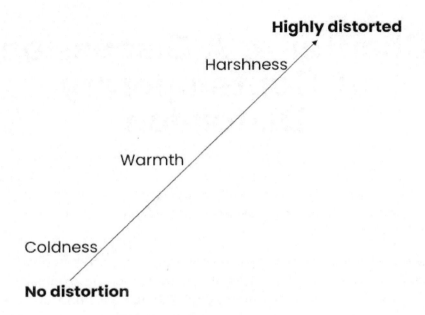

Highly distorted

Harshness

Warmth

Coldness

No distortion

Figure 4.1: Distortion exists on a continuum.

Even if you intend to produce a 'clean', undistorted track, there can be distortive processes that occur between the production of your track and its playback into your listener's ears. Examples include clipping in a microphone recording, analogue equipment in the signal chain, or clipping through a mixer channel or master output.

When a track is finished, distortion can still be added to it, through the mastering process (particularly analogue mastering), and when the music is written to an analogue medium (such as vinyl or tape).

Even once the music is released, distortion can occur at the listener's end. Examples of this include a distortive playback method (such as through an analogue amplifier), distortion by algorithm (such as on a streaming site), or distortion by broadcast, such as compression applied during radio broadcasting.

As you can see, at every stage of the musical process, from creation to playback, more distortion is added – and not all of it is within your control as a music producer. Broadly, the distortion added during production and post-production is considered 'warm' when done correctly, and is often considered a minimum audio standard.

This means, however, that we should consider distortion in terms of two factors: amount – which is how much distortion is added, and intention – which is whether the producer intended for this distortion to occur. This gives us a more nuanced view of contemporary distortion, as shown in Figure 4.2:

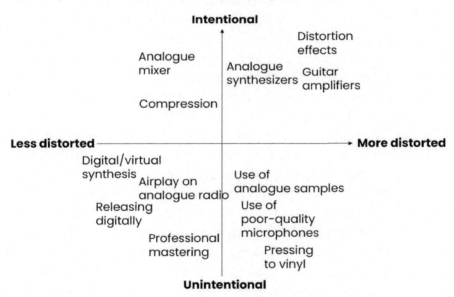

Figure 4.2: Music production and playback techniques along two axes: amount of distortion and intentionality.

As we can see, the addition of distortion to music is a process that occurs throughout the process of music production.

Don't interpret this fact as a reason not to use distortion in your music, however – just bear in mind that distortion is ubiquitous, and not all of it is within your control.

If the goal of contemporary artistry was to capture reality in the cleanest possible manner, many of today's most popular trends wouldn't exist. Guitar amplifiers wouldn't have a 'distortion' pot, top music studios wouldn't have analogue desks, and analogue synthesizers would have been completely replaced by their digital counterparts.

However, that's not the case. In fact, the imperfections of distortion are desirable. Let us explore some reasons.

1. Subtle distortion adds warmth. It's almost a requirement these days to add some small form of distortion to music, whether that's slight saturation on a synthesizer or lead, or mastering via analogue gear. Even though computers have given us an opportunity to write music with minimal distortion, some distortion is what we expect as listeners.

2. Certain types of distortion add temporal character. If you look through a family album of photographs, you'll *feel* the period in which they were captured. You may feel a sense of nostalgia, even hear the voices of family members, or smell the smells of their houses. Equally, a period can be invoked musically by using distortion to call upon a different era. Think of how you can hear a piece of music on the radio and identify the decade in which it was made. Distorted synthesizer pads can call back the 1980s, distorted Fender Rhodes keyboards can call back the 1970s, and a distorted female vocal, sung with a certain style, can call back the 1930s. To dial into these eras, all we need to do is work out how that distortion occurred and recreate it.

3. Distortion can be expressive. Intentionally adding imperfection to distort a cleanly recorded sound can give listeners information about the emotion of the track. An example of this can be found in contemporary hip-hop, where producers distort vocals to create a gritty, unpolished sound, as in Sheck Wes' *Mo Bamba*.

4. When combined with a particular playing style, distortion can contribute to a signature sound. Jimi Hendrix's use of distortion partners with his use of effects and exceptional skill to create a sound that is indelibly his. Think about how easily identifiable a Hendrix track is – even though he was an exceptional guitar player, some of his signature sound came from his unique ways of using distortion. A Hendrix track would be less recognisable played on acoustic guitar.

There are certain rules that govern the use of reverb, delay or compression – and breaking these rules sounds bad to your listeners. Distortion, however, is more subjective, less rule-driven, and as a music producer, it's up to your taste as to how much and what types you wish to use.

Now that we've looked at what distortion is, how it works and what to consider when using it, let's explore, in depth, some contemporary distortion plugins, so that you can use distortion in your own work.

Chapter 5: Contemporary Distortion Types

In this chapter, we will look in more depth at popular contemporary distortion types, analysing how various plugin types add warmth and character to your sound, as well as evaluating the differences between them.

Let's take a moment to consider how to analyse what this plugin does to a signal. Because it's a distortion plugin, we can assume that its main goal is to add harmonics. Therefore, we need to start with a sound that contains little to no harmonics. We also need to choose a low frequency, so that we may easily identify which harmonics pop up when it is used. On this basis, I've selected a 100Hz sine wave. A sine wave, as you'll recall, contains no harmonics, and 100Hz means that we can easily use a frequency spectrum analyser to decipher which harmonics are being activated. For this, I've used MeldaProduction's fantastic MAnalyzer, available at **www.meldaproduction.com**.

On that basis, let's have a look at the spectrum analyser in Figure 5.1 when using a 100Hz sine wave alone, with no additions:

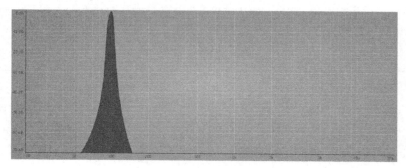

As we can see, the 100Hz sine wave does indeed appear on the frequency analyser with no other harmonics present, and it appears on the oscilloscope as a pure sine wave. This means we're ready to analyse how distortion affects the signal.

Analogue-emulating Distortion

Analogue emulating distortion is the most common type of distortion plugin. It aims to emulate, through its algorithms, tube and valve distortion.

You'll likely find the following features on analogue-emulating plugins:

- *Drive* defines the amplitude of sound driven into the virtual analogue circuit. You'll recall that the higher the input amplitude, the more the valves and tubes are overdriven, and therefore, the more distortion occurs.
- The *Meter* shows the amplitude going through the plugin. This can be represented as a bar that fills as the amplitude increases, virtual lights that glow more strongly depending on the amount of distortion, or perhaps a virtual meter with a needle that moves according to the amplitude. Regardless of the method, the *meter* will make clear the amount of distortion being applied.
- The *Frequency* defines how the distortion behaves at different frequency ranges. At a high level of *Drive*, distortion can obliterate low frequencies and high frequencies. This parameter mitigates this effect, allowing you to maintain your chosen frequency range.
- *Trim*, or *Input* allows you to alter the level of the input.
- *Algorithm* lets you decide which saturation algorithm to use.

- *Output level* determines the amplitude of the output from the plugin.
- *Crosstalk level* determines how much the stereo channels feed into one another.

Let's explore some examples of analogue-emulating distortion in action. Remember we're starting from a lone 100Hz sine wave.

First, let's look at analogue-emulating saturation at a middling amount of *Drive*, while illustrating the harmonics. The result is shown in Figure 5.2:

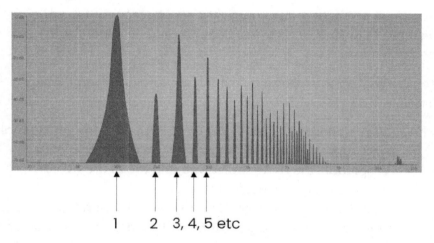

1   2   3, 4, 5 etc

Figure 5.2: Harmonics emerging on an analogue saturation simulating plugin.

As you can see, both odd and even harmonics have emerged, and the waveform on the oscilloscope has changed from a sine wave to a curvy sine wave – closer to a square wave.

Now let's observe analogue-emulating distortion at a high level of *Drive* in Figure 5.3:

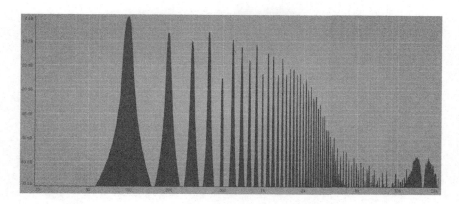

Figure 5.3: Analogue-emulating saturation at a high level of Drive.

You can see that this adds a large amount of odd and even harmonics. You will find that your results vary depending on which plugin you use. This is where your subjectivity as a producer comes in – it's not necessarily the case of one plugin creating *better* distortion than the other; it's up to you as a producer to decide which one fits your sound best.

Another feature of analogue-emulating plugins is that their response depends on the amplitude of the input signal. Higher amplitude input signals leave less headroom and therefore generate more distortion. On the top of Figure 5.4, I'll show a typical plugin's frequency response to a normal-level sine wave, and on the bottom, I'll show its frequency response to a lower amplitude sine wave.

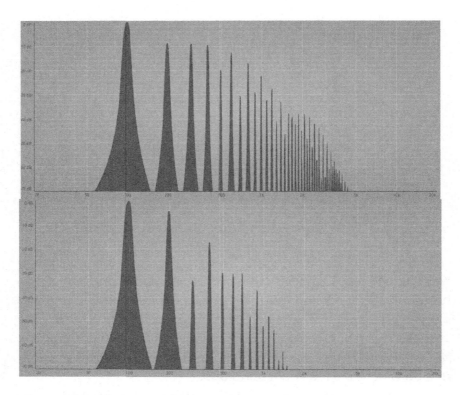

Figure 5.4: Above: A high-amplitude sine wave. Below: a low amplitude sine wave. Both are adjusted for amplitude, showing the effect of the distortion only.

As you can see, the output of analogue-emulating saturation plugins depends a great deal on their input level. In fact, many plugin creators advise that, for optimal results, the input signal should reach around 0dB; so many plugins offer a *Trim* parameter, so that you may alter the input amplitude of the signal without having to fiddle with the amplitude of plugins prior to the distortion in the signal chain.

Finally, let's explore two different algorithms on a typical analogue-emulating saturation plugin – one that emphasises low frequencies, and another that emphasises high frequencies.

Figure 5.5 shows the results of a low frequency algorithm:

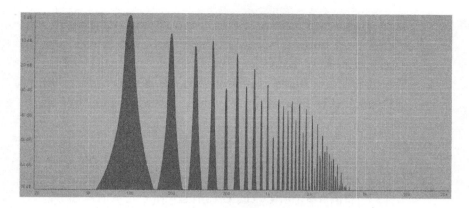

Figure 5.5 A lower frequency emphasising algorithm.

As you can see, the lower frequencies have been enhanced, with more emphasis on the fundamental. It sounds fuller.

Figure 5.6 shows a high frequency algorithm in use:

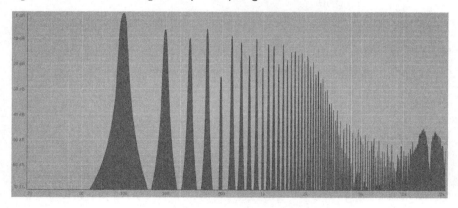

Figure 5.6: A higher frequency emphasising algorithm.

As seen, the fundamental frequency has dropped slightly, but a lot of energy between 4kHz and 20kHz has been added. It sounds sharper.

Let's therefore summarise what we've learned about analogue-emulating distortion:

- Analogue emulation adds a lot of odd and even harmonic content, emulating hardware distortion well. This is likely to result in a warm sound.
- The amount of distortion depends not only upon the value of *Drive*, but the input level, which can often be controlled using *Trim*.
- *Frequency* is a key parameter, in that:
    o Low frequency distortion keeps the bottom end when the amount of distortion is pushed higher.
    o High frequency distortion sacrifices some of the bottom end but adds a lot of harmonics in the high frequency range.
    o Middling distortion adds a lot of energy in the central frequency range, although some of the bass falls away when the amount of distortion is pushed higher.

Now that we've analysed analogue emulation, let's look at a less common, but growing form of distortion: waveshaping.

Waveshaping

Whilst analogue-emulating distortion often involves some amount of waveshaping hidden within its algorithms, some plugins are explicitly built around waveshaping, such as Ableton Live's Saturator.

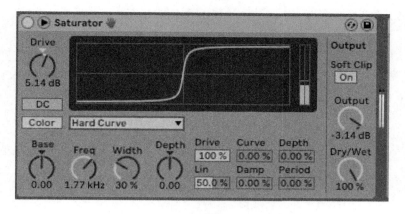

Figure 5.7: Ableton Live's Saturator.

The difference between analogue-emulating distortion and waveshaping is that whereas analogue emulation tries to recreate the warmth, the quirks, and the joy of analogue distortion, waveshaping tries to be as transparent as possible, offering the user a great deal of control.

Let's analyse some features commonly seen in waveshapers:

- *Drive* allows you to change the level of the input signal as it enters the plugin. This is an important parameter, because we know that, given the non-linearities of saturation, this can vary the amount of saturation applied.
- *Shape* allows you to select or generate a waveshaper curve. How you select or generate a waveshape can vary, depending on the plugin you use – but we shall explore some common wave shapes in this chapter.
- *Output* allows you to choose the output level of the audio from the plugin.
- *Dry/Wet* allows you to specify how much of the audio signal you wish to be processed by the distortion unit. 100% *Wet* is the saturated signal in its entirety; 50% *Wet* is a 50/50 mix of the saturated (*Wet*) and unsaturated (*Dry*) signals; 0% *Wet* (or 100% *Dry*) means none of the saturated signal comes through the output.

Let's examine how some common waveshapes affect a 100Hz sine wave.

First, let's explore a fairly gentle shape in Figure 5.8:

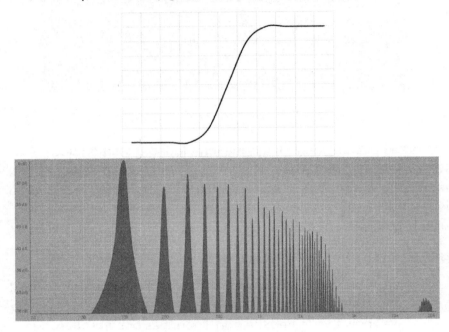

Figure 5.8: A gentle waveshape used on a 100Hz sine wave.

As you can see, the gentle curves of the waveshape have generated both odd and even harmonics, with a gentle roll-off of frequencies, ending around 3kHz. This is likely to sound crunchy and warm.

Next, let's look at the results of a harsh waveshape in Figure 5.9:

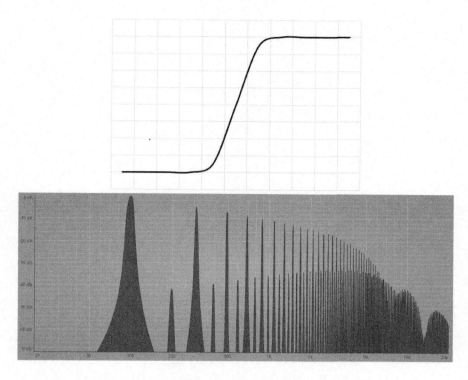

Figure 5.9: A harsh clipping waveshape and its results.

As we can see, this has led to a far higher presence of odd harmonics than even harmonics. The frequency roll-off is much higher, with harmonics being generated to 20kHz. There is a second, small peak around 16kHz. This is likely to generate cold, harsh, ringing distortion.

Now, let's explore a softer, horizontal curve in Figure 5.10:

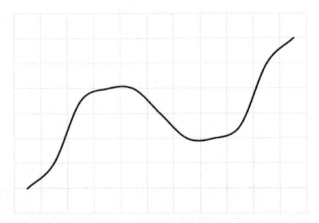

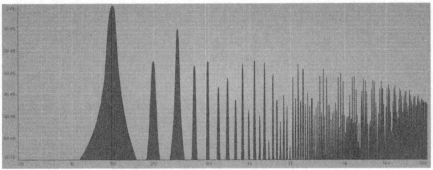

Figure 5.10: A softer horizontal curve waveshape and its results.

This curve has created odd and even harmonics, with a very slow roll-off of frequencies. This distortion is likely to sound warm once the harsh high frequency content is filtered out.

Finally, let's explore an asymmetric, tube-like curve in Figure 5.11:

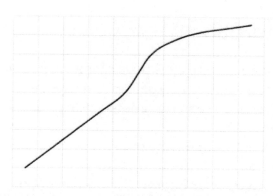

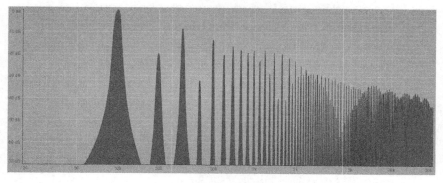

Figure 5.11: An asymmetric waveshape and its result.

This has generated odd and even harmonics, with a far higher harmonic presence in the mid frequency range than other waveshapes. This is likely to sound warm and inviting once the harsh top end is filtered out. As we can see, waveshaping is a helpful form of saturation if you want a high amount of control over the result. However, if you are simply looking for distortion that sounds good, and you don't want to delve into the specifics of waveshaping, an analogue-emulating plugin may be more suitable.

Next, let's look at a form of saturation that has increased in popularity over the last few years: tape saturation.

Tape Saturation

- Tape saturation plugins have gained in popularity recently, driven partly by a resurgence in the synthesizer music of the 1980s. Common parameters within tape saturation plugins include:
- *Drive*, which controls the amount of saturation applied to the signal.
- *Noise,* which adds a tape hiss to your sound.
- *Wow* adds subtle frequency modulation caused by slight changes in the speed of the tape motors.
- *Flutter* creates frequency changes caused by the tape's movements as it moves across the playback head.
- *Speed* defines the speed at which the tape crosses the heads. It is measured in *IPS*, meaning inches per second. A higher speed means a higher-fidelity sound, as there's more tape per second to write onto. Therefore, producers who are trying to distort their sound using tape aim for a lower IPS number, often 7.5IPS.
- *Bias* is an ultrasonic signal that helps maximise the tape's fidelity. Some producers enjoy over-biasing the sound to create intentional degradation.
- *Algorithm* allows you to choose which type of simulated tape is employed.
- *Oversampling* allows you to oversample a signal. You'll recall the process of downsampling distortion in Chapters 1 and 2; oversampling is the opposite. Oversampling means the plugin captures extra frames of audio to manipulate high frequencies in more detail. The higher the amount of oversampling, the better the quality of distortion. However, this better quality comes at the expense of your processing power, meaning your computer has less capacity to process other layers of your track.
- *Output gain* allows you to select the output level of the plugin.

The results depend on the plugin, but tape saturation tends to create mostly or exclusively odd-order harmonics, as shown in Figure 5.12:

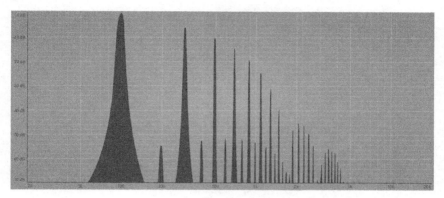

Figure 5.12: Tape saturation creates mostly odd-order harmonics.

Many tape distortion plugins include a *Noise* parameter.

Whilst this noise is not inherently distortive, producers may find this noise to add a characteristic hiss on more analogue-sounding tracks, which can be atmospheric when hidden in the mix at a very low amplitude.

Next, let's have a look at the *Wow* parameter.

Wow simulates the imperfections of the tape's motor. This sounds like the frequency of the sound increasing and decreasing rapidly, as if an LFO was used. This is shown in Figure 5.13:

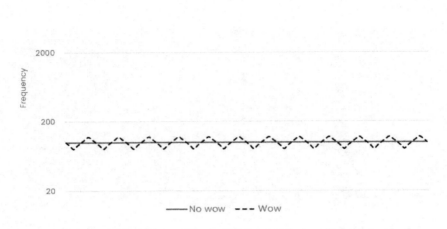

Figure 5.13: A comparison of a 100Hz sine wave without Wow and a 100Hz sine wave with Wow applied.

Wow is a useful effect when used subtly. It can make melodies sound warmer, especially in retro genres such as Vaporwave.

The next parameter to investigate is Flutter.

Flutter is caused by irregular tape motion during playback. This causes an inharmonic buzz, visualised in Figure 5.14:

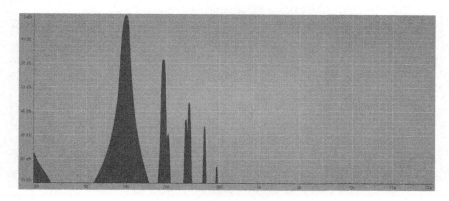

Figure 5.14: The inharmonic buzz generated by the Flutter parameter.

As seen, whereas the usual harmonic profile of saturation is multiples of the fundamental frequency (100hz), these harmonics are roughly 90% of the fundamental frequency. Whilst too much of this effect sounds unpleasant, a small amount of it can create a subtle grit that can enhance a melodic sound.

Speed makes a slight difference to the higher frequency harmonics. This is a parameter best left until last and experimented with by ear, as comparing a spectrum analysis of various *Speed* settings will yield almost identical results.

Low *Bias* tends to add harmonics to the mid-range of the tape saturation, known as 'dead zone' distortion. Where this occurs, lower frequencies are reduced in amplitude, leading to the distorted sound seeming slightly weaker and more distant from the listener. This is shown in Figure 5.15:

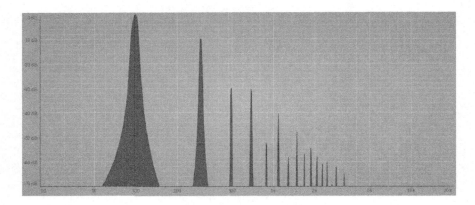

Figure 5.15: The spectrum analysis of low bias.

High *Bias* leads to a gentler saturation profile, as seen in Figure 5.16:

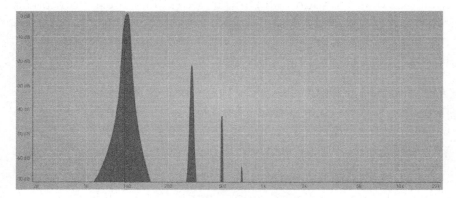

Figure 5.16: The spectrum analysis of high bias.

Many tape distortion plugins have a selection of algorithms available, modelled on different tapes. Two are compared in Figure 5.17:

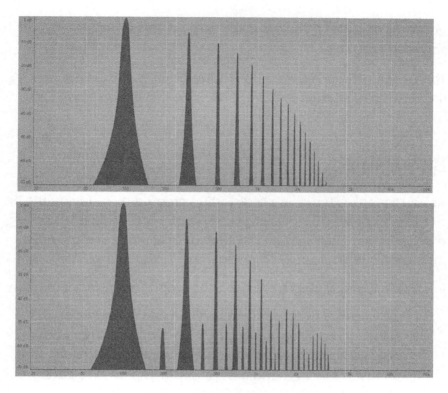

Figure 5.17: Two tape algorithms compared.

As shown, the top profile has no even harmonics, but has a smoother roll-off of frequencies. The bottom profile is slightly more harmonically rich, but with less mid frequency content. This would have a more 'vintage' sound.

Let's summarise what we've learned about tape distortion:

- Tape distortion is often composed of mostly odd harmonics.
- Tape has some inharmonic distortive features, such as *Wow* and *Flutter*. These can add a 'vintage' feel to a sound.

It's therefore reasonable to surmise that if you want basic distortion, tape distortion may not be the best place to start. However, tape will do a great job if you want something retro, or quirky – especially if you're looking to give an element like a lead some added edge.

This concludes our exploration of tape distortion. The next, and final form of distortion that we shall explore is *Bitcrushing*.

Bitcrushing

As you'll recall, bitcrushing is distortion created by reducing the bit depth and/or the sample rate of a sound. Bitcrushing is becoming more prevalent in music production, as producers seek novel, inharmonic effects.

In any bitcrushing plugin, the two most important parameters are:

- *Bit depth*, which is the implied number of audio values within a recorded waveform. A 32-bit depth implies over four million values, a 16-bit depth implies over sixty-five thousand values, and a 4-bit depth implies only sixteen values.
- *Sample rate* is the implied number of audio samples taken per second. Within this plugin, this is measured as a fraction, with the parameter changing the denominator of the fraction. The lowest value is /1, which divides the sample rate by 1 and therefore has no effect. The highest value depends on the plugin but can range from around 128 to 512.

These two parameters are illustrated in Figure 5.18:

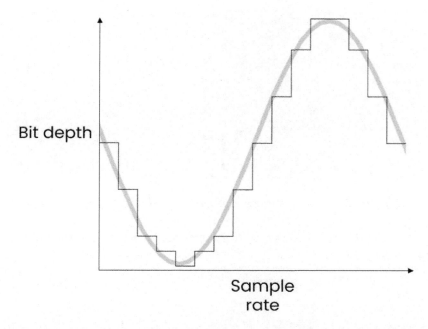

Figure 5.18: Bit depth and sample rate described graphically.

The setting to start with on any bitcrusher is a *bit depth* of 16 and a *sample rate* of /0. This means that the audio has its highest bit depth, and the sample rate is not being divided. Therefore, the plugin has no effect on the sound.

At a *bit depth* of 8 (i.e., dividing it by two), harmonics emerge, as shown in Figure 5.19:

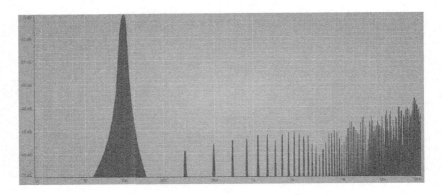

Figure 5.19: Harmonics generated at a bit depth of 8.

At a *bit depth* of 4, these harmonics are extremely prominent, as seen in Figure 5.20:

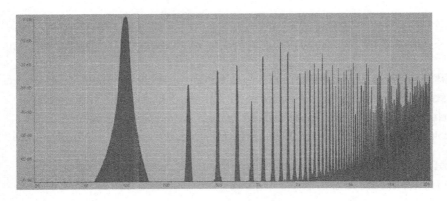

Figure 5.20: Harmonics generated by a bit depth of 4.

At a *bit depth* of 2 (i.e., divided by 8), the harmonics are exceptionally strong, as shown in Figure 5.21:

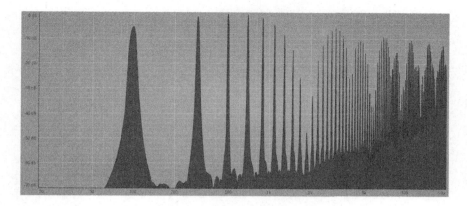

Figure 5.21: Harmonics generated at a bit depth of 2.

Reduction of the sample rate also creates non-harmonic overtones.

A 100Hz sine wave, downsampled slightly, is shown in Figure 5.22:

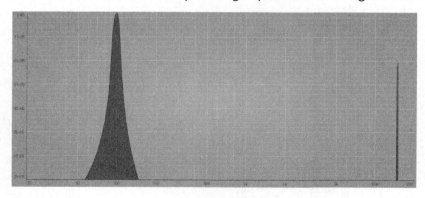

Figure 5.22: A 100Hz sine wave with a small amount of downsampling.

As you can see, a harmonic has popped up. However, this harmonic is around 14.5kHz. We're used to seeing odd or even harmonics, which are multiples of the fundamental, however this one seems to bear no mathematical relation to the fundamental. In fact, this harmonic persists even if the fundamental is changed to 50Hz. This shows that this is an artefact of the process of sample rate reduction itself.

Further downsampling is shown in Figure 5.23:

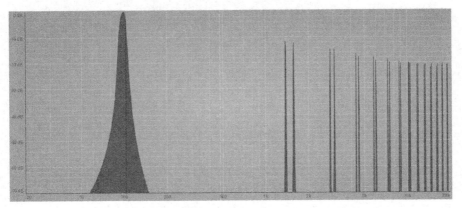

Figure 5.23: The sample rate divided by 16.

You can now see several non-harmonic artefacts occurring at higher frequencies.

Finally, Figure 5.24 shows the results of harsh downsampling:

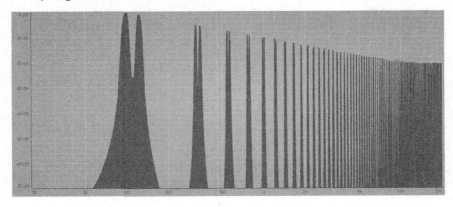

Figure 5.24: Harsh downsampling

At a sample rate this low, the entire signal degrades, and even the fundamental is lost.

As you can see, degrading the sample rate means that fewer frames of audio can be captured per second, so the signal itself loses clarity.

However, whilst a 100Hz test signal is perfect for conducting a scientific analysis of the effects of bitcrushing, the results are so odd and non-harmonic that it's worth testing it on a real sound.

For example, Figure 5.25 is the frequency analysis of a standard pad:

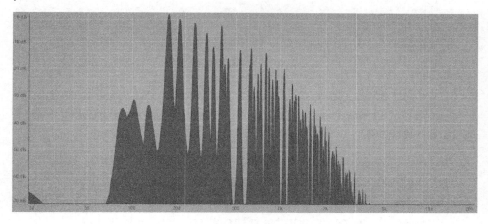

Figure 5.25: The frequency analysis of a pad sound.

However, when a bitcrusher is applied, with moderate bit reduction and light downsampling, non-harmonic overtones are added. This is shown in Figure 5.26:

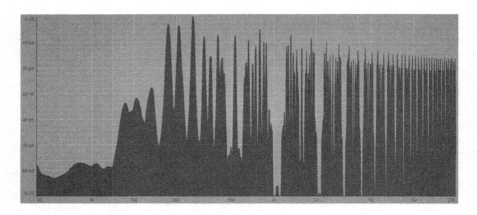

Figure 5.26: The bitcrusher has generated non-harmonic overtones.

This adds an artificial sheen onto the pad sound – one that should sound poor but gives the pad some sharpness and draws attention to it.

This defies logic – harmonics sound good, and therefore non-harmonic noise should not. However, this is the magic of bitcrushing – subtle amounts of it can transform your sound, and it is useful if you're aiming for a brash sound, such as in an EDM lead.

In summary:

- Bitcrushing distortion tends to be inharmonic. This shouldn't work, but it does!
- The sound is less warm and enveloping than traditional analogue emulation – it is fascinating and chaotic.
- When the sample rate is low enough, bitcrushing causes a significant breakdown in the sound, making it bear little resemblance to the input signal.

This concludes the analysis of the types of distortion you're most likely to happen across.

A summary of these types of distortion is in Table 5.1:

Table 5.1: A summary of different types of distortion plugins.

Type of distortion simulated	Complexity	Examples
Analog	Moderate	Saturation Knob, IVGI
Waveshaping/analog	Complex	Ableton Saturator, AudioThing Wavebox
Tape	Moderate	Caelum Audio Tape Cassette, Chowdhury DSP ChowTape
Bitcrushing	Moderate	Ableton Redux, TAL-Bitcrusher

In the next chapter, let's look at the use of distortion in your own music production. In the meantime, however, here are some exercises that may help you get used to distortion.

Recommended Exercises

1. If you own a DAW, find its built-in saturation modules.
2. Using each of these, conduct your own experiment, using a single sine wave and a spectrum analyser to find out what harmonics these plugins are emphasising. .

Chapter 6: Tips for Using Distortion

Now that you understand what distortion plugins do to your sound, let's look at how to use them best.

As we've already discussed in Chapter 3, there are boundaries when using many effects plugins, and if you move outside these boundaries, your music will suffer. When using distortion, these boundaries are far fewer, and you are freer to explore the limits of the effect.

However, this chapter will provide the fundamental principles that you should always remember if you wish to use distortion effectively in your work.

A Basic Workflow

Should you wish to add distortion as an insert effect (i.e. on a single track alone), the workflow is simple.

1. Add the distortion plugin to the track you wish to distort. Be careful if you have other insert effects such as reverb or delay within this signal chain. If you add the distortion before a reverb, for example, the reverb will reverberate the distorted signal. If you add the distortion after a reverb, the reverb will reverberate a clean signal, to be later distorted by the distortion. A distortion at the end of the effects chain is my preference, as it leaves delay and reverb tails sounding 'cleaner', but experiment with both options.
2. Turn *Drive* just beyond the point where you think it sounds good, then dial back from there.

3. Adjust the *Frequency* parameter according to which areas of the frequency spectrum you wish to keep.

There is, of course, more nuance to this workflow – such as plugin choice, use of *Dry/Wet*, the use of EQ, and the use of parallel processing to split your distortion. We will explore this nuance within this chapter.

Plugin Choice

Just like many instruments and effects, plugin choice matters. Each distortion plugin is unique, and each has its own unique sonic character.

It is therefore worth gaining several distortion plugins. As a starting point, I would consider:

- Two or three analogue-simulating distortion plugins.
- A tape distortion plugin.
- A bitcrushing plugin.
- A vintage compressor.
- A vinyl distortion plugin (optional).

It is perfectly reasonable to use free plugins. Many are of great quality – and you can always explore a company's paid products if you fall in love with their free plugins.

Once you've downloaded the plugins, get to know them well. You'll find that analogue-simulating plugins have a great deal of detail.

There are so many choices when choosing which plugin to use on a particular sound that it's easy to experience choice paralysis. I suggest you experiment in depth with your plugins to understand the effect that each has on your sound, but I'll provide a starting point in Table 6.1:

Table 6.1: Starting points to consider, depending on your requirements.

You want	Consider
Subtle warmth	Tube simulation
Brash warmth	Tube simulation
Extreme distortion	Bitcrushing
Extra presence	Tube simulation/Digital distortion
Filtered warmth	Tape saturation
Crunchy warmth	Vinyl simulation
Cold crunchiness	Digital distortion/bitcrushing
Vintage 1980s sound	Tape saturation

A/B Testing and Levels

When you've added distortion to a track, you may find it difficult to judge how much distortion is the right amount.

On this basis, I recommend pushing the distortion to the limits of what seems sensible, usually using the *Drive* parameter, then dialling it back from there. From there, you can do an A/B test, by turning the distortion off and on again (or to *Bypass* and back to *On* in some DAWs) to see what effect it's had on your track. The *Off* (or *Bypass*) button is shown in Figure 6.1:

Off button

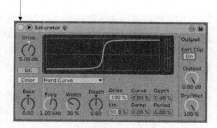

Figure 6.1: The Off button in Ableton Live's Saturator, which bypasses the plugin.

Although distortion is an effect that originates in pushing audio equipment to its limits, that doesn't mean that your sound will maintain the same level throughout the distortion process. Different degrees of *Drive* will change the amplitude of the sound.

As human beings, we naturally perceive louder music to sound better. This is why the music in clubs sounds so good. It also makes it easy to make mistakes when using distortion, as your judgement of the effect of the distortion can be blinded by increases or decreases in volume. For example, compare these three examples in Figure 6.2 of the volume of a sound distorted using analogue-emulating saturation:

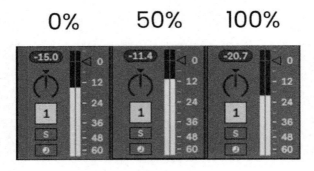

Figure 6.2: Different degrees of distortion can have a drastic effect on your channel's amplitude.

As you can see, the level of the sound without distortion is -15dB. However, when *Drive* is 50% of the way up, this level increases to -11.4dB, then at 100% it decreases all the way to -20.7dB.

Therefore, when using distortion, you may wish to use a tool such as Ableton's Utility to compensate for any changes in level because of your distortion. For example, if I were to set *Drive* to 50%, I would analyse the change in gain using the mixer's meter and change the *Gain* within Ableton's utility to compensate for this so that the level stayed the same. This is shown in Figure 6.3:

Figure 6.3: Ableton Live's Utility can compensate for an increase in amplitude.

Equally, you should be aware of your sound's dynamic range, which is the difference between the quietest sounds and the loudest sounds. Compare these two examples in Figure 6.4 of a sound before and after saturation:

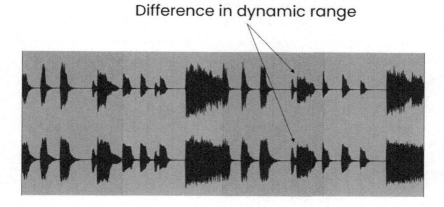

Figure 6.4: An example of dynamic range, visualised in Ableton Live.

As you can see, in the bottom waveform, the loudest sounds have stayed at a similar level, but the quietest sounds have increased in level. This means that the dynamic range has reduced.

This often isn't a problem in distortion, because you distort sounds that are at the front and centre of your mix, such as electric guitars, leads or vocals. However, it's worth bearing this dynamic range reduction in mind when working with instruments like the human voice, pianos, or acoustic drum kits – instruments that derive their expressiveness from dynamics. Here, the corrective action is to listen out for the dynamic range and make sure that it still makes sense as a recording. If not, you may wish to consider distorting in parallel, which we will get to at the end of this chapter.

To summarise, push *Drive* until it sounds too distorted, then bring it back from there to a comfortable level. Make sure, however, you keep the levels the same, or you may think something sounds better when all that's happened is that it's louder.

Dry/Wet or Less Distortion?

The most common form of distortion that I apply to my work is not the aggressive type, but a subtle warming up of a sound. This leads to an interesting question: is it better to add a large amount of distortion applied subtly using *Dry/Wet*, or is it better to add a small amount of distortion to the whole signal at 100% *Wet?*

Let's compare the two. The top of Figure 6.5 shows gentle saturation at 100% *Wet*, with the bottom showing harsh saturation at 25% *Wet*:

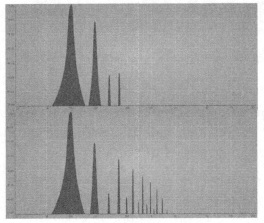

Gentle saturation, 100% Wet

Harsh saturation, 25% Wet

Figure 6.5: Two distortion types and Wet/Dry amounts compared.

Let's compare the two sets of harmonics.

As you can see, the gentle saturation at 100% *Wet* has created a far greater amount of second harmonics, whereas the harsh saturation has created a far greater number of higher harmonics (around the 2-3kHz mark).

The difference is that the gentle saturation is a consequence of the virtual audio circuit being overdriven slightly, whereas the 25%

Wet saturation is the virtual audio circuit being overdriven significantly, but at a quarter of the amplitude.

The gentle saturation at 100% *Wet* sounds warmer, more inviting and more natural. The harsh saturation at 25% *Wet* sounds brighter, but more muted and less natural.

This means for you, as a producer, that if you wish to add subtle distortion, tend towards adding a large amount of soft distortion, not a small amount of harsh distortion. Soft distortion sounds more natural, warmer, and more inviting.

There are exceptions, however. If you wish for your sound to be hollower (for example, if you're writing an aggressive dubstep bass), then a small amount of harsh distortion may do the trick.

Next, let's explore how EQ can enhance your use of distortion.

Using EQ with Distortion

We've already established that distortion adds harmonics to a signal. Invariably, the addition of this audio information can change the implications of mixing that part. Compare the two spectrum analyses of a pad sound before and after distortion in Figure 6.6:

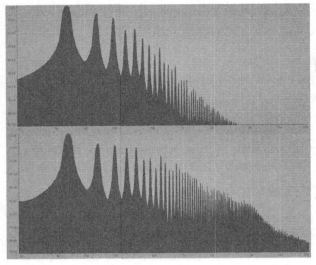

Before distortion

After distortion

Figure 6.6: A bass before and after distortion.

As you can see, the distortion has added some sub-bass frequencies below 100Hz and increased the body of the harmonics from 800Hz upwards.

Because this is a pad with a fundamental frequency around 160Hz, the extra sub-bass energy added to this pad sound is of no use. It doesn't sound good and will merely occupy sonic space that should be occupied by instruments intended for the sub-bass range, such as the kick drum. Therefore, we may wish to consider the use of parametric EQ to shape the sound.

EQ is a great tool when working with distortion, as it can help you shape the timbre of your distorted sound. To use EQ with distortion, tend to add the EQ plugin after your distortion plugin.

An example of this is shown in Figure 6.7, where a high-pass filter has been used to remove needless sub-bass frequencies.

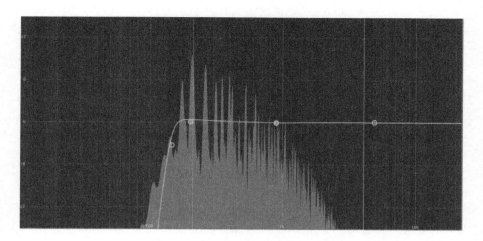

Figure 6.7: EQ Eight added in Ableton Live to remove the sub-bass added by distortion.

The next step is to listen to the harmonics that have been added.

You can do this by setting the Q of a frequency notch on your EQ as high as possible, then increasing the level of this notch to a high degree, say +12dB, as shown in Figure 6.8:

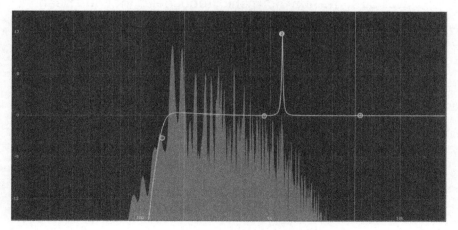

Figure 6.8: Setting a high, specific notch on Ableton Live's EQ Eight.

You can then move this notch up and down to highlight problem frequencies. You'll hear them as a harsh, resonant ring. Just make sure you turn down the level of your headphones or speakers before you do this, otherwise your ears will suffer!

What you may find is that, whereas your lower harmonics are aligned with the notes of your instrument, you may hear non-harmonic frequencies as you ascend the frequency spectrum. This is because whilst lower-level overtones such as second, third, fifth and seventh harmonics sound lush, when you get to much higher levels of harmonics, the frequencies don't correlate as cleanly with the fundamentals.

Therefore, you have two options:

1. You could use high Q values to reduce the level of problem areas. Q is short for *Quality*, and it allows you to select a wide or narrow band to EQ. A narrow band is more precise, but can sound unnatural when used too harshly, whereas a wide band is less precise, but can sound more natural. A higher Q value means a narrower band. In Figure 6.9 below, I've reduced the level of some areas that sounded fuzzy, as well as some non-harmonic frequencies that had been introduced:

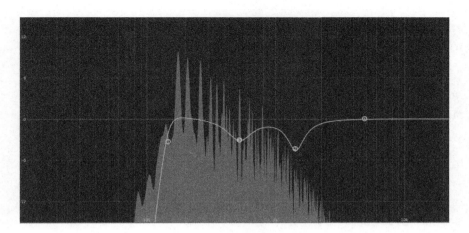

Figure 6.9: Reducing the level of problem areas using Ableton Live's EQ Eight.

2. You could use several notches with very high *Q* values to specifically target the problem frequencies that you find, as shown in Figure 6.10:

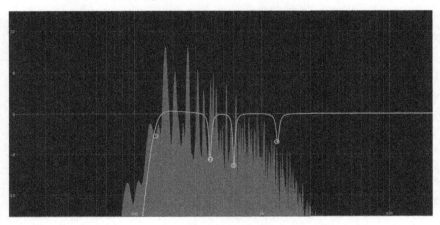

Figure 6.10: Using several notches with very high Q values to reduce the amplitude of problem frequencies, using Ableton Live's EQ Eight.

Both methods have their value. You may even find it optimal to combine the two: an initial precise elimination of problematic frequencies followed by a milder EQ when you work on your final mix.

To summarise, adding distortion adds audio information as harmonics. Most of this audio information is desirable, but I strongly recommend searching for and eliminating any of this audio information that is undesirable.

In the next and final section of this chapter, we will explore how you can harness the best of both worlds – the cleanliness of the original sound and the harmonic warmth of distortion – using parallel processing.

Parallel Processing

One of the main challenges you'll encounter when working with distortion is using it with precision. Distortion tends to have a disproportionate effect on your lowest and highest frequencies. We've looked at this to some extent in this chapter, where we compared the use of gentle distortion curves to the use of harsh distortion with *Dry/Wet*. We've also considered that in some plugins, this is mitigated by selecting an algorithm (using the *Frequency* parameter) that emphasises your lowest or highest frequencies.

However, if you're working with key elements of your track, you may need to split a single track into distorted and undistorted elements.

For example, what if you wished to distort the harmonics of your kick drum to create fuzz and grit, but leave the fundamentals untouched to maintain the kick's power? This is visualised in Figure 6.11:

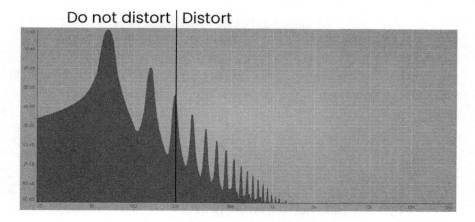

Figure 6.11: Attempting to distort frequencies above 200Hz only.

Alternatively, what if you wished to only distort sounds above a certain amplitude, as shown in Figure 6.12?

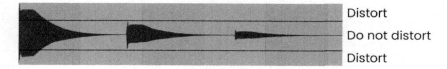

Figure 6.12: Attempting to distort sounds above a particular amplitude only. Visualised using Ableton Live.

The answer to this is parallel processing. Let's explore some parallel processing techniques.

Filtering

If you wish to distort certain frequencies, you will need to separate these from the source. A useful way to do this is using an **auxiliary track** (often shortened to aux track). An aux track is a mixer track you can pass audio to, but you can't record any audio or MIDI to it. It is often used by producers looking to apply the same effect to multiple mixer channels. You can send a chosen amount of the audio signal to the aux track using a control called *Send*.

A diagram of the signal flow of an aux channel is shown in Figure 6.13. This shows the output from three tracks being routed to an aux track, to which an effect has been assigned. The output of this aux track, together with the individual outputs of the three tracks themselves, then converge upon the main output, as shown in Figure 6.13:

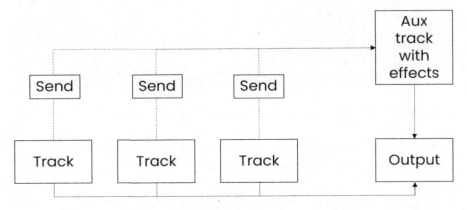

Figure 6.13: Routing three tracks to an aux track.

Using *Send*, you can send a differing amount of each track to the aux track, as shown in Figure 6.14:

Aux track

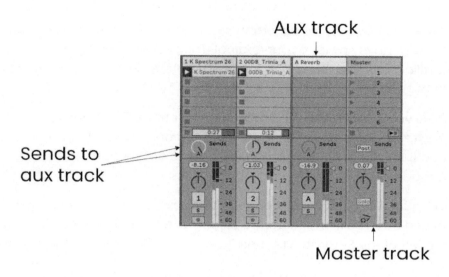

Sends to aux track

Master track

Figure 6.14: Sending tracks to an aux track in Ableton Live.

You can use this for distortion by sending some of your track to an auxiliary track with a distortion plugin.

To create and send an aux track yourself, complete the following steps:

1. Create an auxiliary track (known as a *Return* track in Ableton Live).
2. Use the *Send* parameter on your mixer to 'send' one of your mixer tracks to this auxiliary channel. Here, set *Send* to its maximum amount.
3. Add a distortion plugin to the auxiliary track you have created.

However, you may notice that if you send a track fully to an auxiliary track, you will now have two simultaneous signals coming through your master output: your original track, together with your distorted auxiliary track. This duplicate copy can lead to unwanted distortion, because it increases the amplitude of audio coming through your master output.

If the *Dry/Wet* on your distortion plugin is set to less than 100%, you will also have some of your original track coming through your auxiliary track (as the *Dry* portion). Therefore, set your distortion to 100% *Wet*.

Next, you need to filter your distortion aux track. This is so that only the frequencies you want to be distorted are distorted. This is because you want the distortion plugin to act only on the frequencies you feed it.

In Figure 6.15 below, only frequencies above 200Hz will be received by the aux track, and therefore distorted. Notice how the EQ is to the left of the Saturator, putting it before the Saturator in the signal chain:

Figure 6.15: A plugin configuration that distorts frequencies above 200Hz only.

However, you may have spotted something. With this filter in place, your original sound will be mixed with everything above 200Hz on your auxiliary track – so you're still mixing the original sound with the distortion above 200Hz.

You cannot add a filter to your original sound to filter out everything above 200Hz, otherwise you'll filter out everything you want to distort using the auxiliary track.

The solution is therefore to route your original sound to an additional audio track, so that you can manipulate this audio track and can't hear the original, as seen in Figure 6.16:

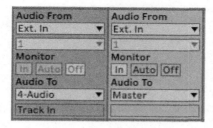

Figure 6.16: Routing the original sound to an additional audio track in Ableton Live.

You could then add a filter in the opposite direction, say under 200Hz. An example of such a filter in Ableton Live is shown in Figure 6.17:

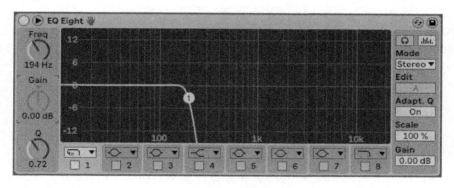

Figure 6.17: A 200Hz filter using Ableton Live's EQ Eight.

This means that you are now splitting your original sound in two directions: frequencies above 200Hz will be distorted by your auxiliary track, and frequencies under 200Hz will be processed as you see fit. This signal flow is shown in Figure 6.18:

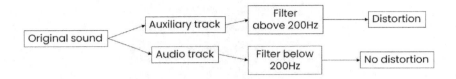

Figure 6.18: A signal flow diagram depicting only frequencies above 200Hz being distorted.

It's also worth noting that there are more and more multiband distortion plugins appearing on the market – these allow you to make these frequency splits within the plugin, applying a separate distortion algorithm to each section.

Let's have a look at a different way of parallel mixing, this time distorting mono content (i.e., the centre of the stereo field), but leaving stereo content at the sides untouched.

Stereo Split

One technique you may wish to attempt, particularly when working with prominent elements such as vocals or a lead, is to split the stereo information of a sound into a distorted and undistorted copy. For example, you may wish for the sound in the centre to be undistorted, but the stereo information (such as a stereo delay, for example) to be distorted.

Assuming you're starting from a mono track, but you wish to add distorted stereo effects (such as reverb or delay), the technique is very similar to splitting by frequency.

1. Route your source signal (such as your lead or vocal) to another audio track (not an aux track). This new audio track will be your mono copy.
2. On this (undistorted) audio track, add a Utility plugin, to sum your signal to mono. If you don't have Ableton Live, your DAW will probably have a plugin to sum to mono – for

example, the Gain plugin in Logic Pro X. In Ableton Live, activate *Mono,* as shown in Figure 6.19. This means that the plugin is summing any lingering stereo information from your source into the centre.

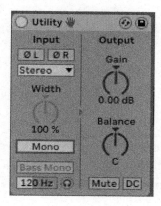

Figure 6.19: Switching Ableton Live's Utility plugin to Mid/Side Mode.

3. Then create an auxiliary track, and add the stereo effects you want, such as Stereo Delay. Make sure that the *Dry/Wet* of these effects is set to 100%. You can then send your original source to this auxiliary track, as seen in Figure 6.20.

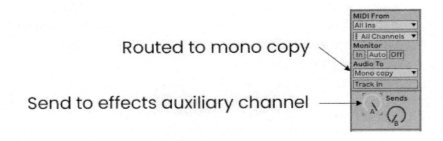

Routed to mono copy

Send to effects auxiliary channel

Figure 6.20: Sending a track to an auxiliary track in Ableton Live.

4. Once you've done this, you can add your distortion to either the start or the end of the auxiliary effects chain. An example is shown in Figure 6.21:

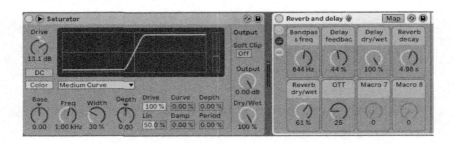

Figure 6.21: Distortion added to the start of an effects chain.

Inevitably, with this technique, there will still be some audio information in the centre, but that's OK – just listen back to your whole mix in Mono to ensure that it all sounds clear. The signal flow is summarised in Figure 6.22:

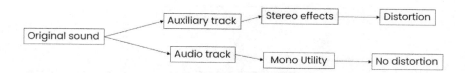

Figure 6.22: The signal flow when splitting by stereo information.

Alternatively, if you wish to leave the stereo effects clean, but the Mono distorted, you can simply invert where you place the distortion. Instead of adding it to the auxiliary track, you can add it to your mono audio track instead, as shown in Figure 6.23:

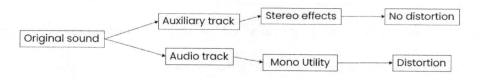

Figure 6.23: An inverted signal flow, where the Mono signal is distorted, but the Stereo signal is left untouched.

Next, let's have a look at distorting sounds above or below a certain audio threshold.

Gate and Compressor Split

You may wish to only apply distortion to the loudest sections of a sound, for example when a vocalist uses emphasis. To split your sound by its level, you can use a device known as a Gate.

A Gate is a device that only allows sounds through if they reach a certain loudness threshold. It drastically attenuates all signals below that threshold. Imagine a threshold applied to a passage of music, like the one shown in Figure 6.24 for example:

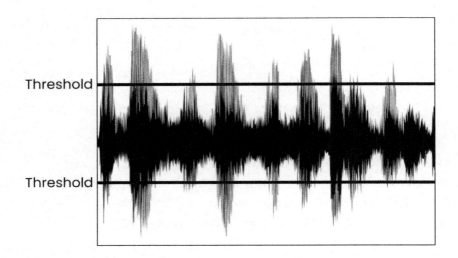

Figure 6.24: An illustration of the threshold of a Gate.

Since a Gate would refuse to let through any audio that didn't meet the threshold, the resulting audio wave would look stuttered, like the one in Figure 6.25:

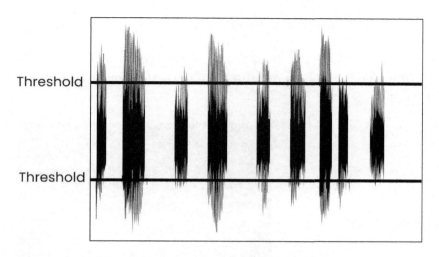

Figure 6.25: An illustration of a sound after the application of Gate.

This Gate technique can only distort sounds above or below a threshold.

Therefore, to create a gated distortion, follow these steps.

1. Send the track that you wish to distort to an auxiliary track with a Gate placed upon it. Play your track and observe the audio levels entering the Gate, as illustrated in Figure 6.26. You can utilise these levels to set the Gate's main parameters correctly.

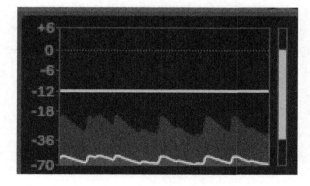

Figure 6.26: The Gate's display, depicted in Ableton Live.

2. *Threshold* sets the level at which the Gate is activated. Set
    this to where you want the Gate to be activated, as shown
    in Figure 6.27.

Threshold ⟶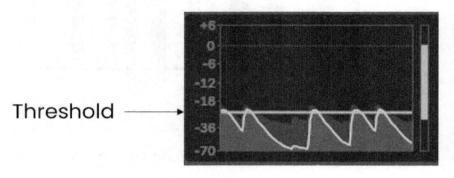

*Figure 6.27: The addition of a Threshold to a Gate in Ableton
Live.*

3. *Return* sets the difference between the level at which the
    Gate is activated and the level at which it is deactivated.
    This is useful when the Gate causes 'chattering' by opening
    and closing too rapidly. For now, you can leave this set to
    0dB.
4. *Floor* defines the baseline amount of audio that the Gate
    passes when it is not active. This is where you can choose
    how much background sound the Gate is passing. You
    should start by setting this to –inf dB so that no sound
    passes. You can see *Floor* in the bottom-right corner of
    Figure 6.28:

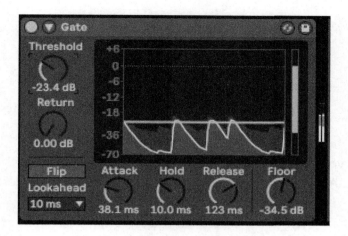

Figure 6.28: Ableton Live's Gate, including the Floor parameter in the bottom-right of the Figure.

5. There are also envelope parameters that you should experiment with:
   ○ *Attack* defines how long it takes the Gate to work after the *Threshold* is breached.
   ○ *Hold* defines how long the Gate continues after the sound dips back below the *Threshold*.
   ○ *Release* defines the sharpness with which the Gate releases, after the Hold phase.

An aggressive *Attack* can create an unnatural, sharp sound. For a Gate to be effective, it's important to create an envelope that also maintains realism. This requires a longer *Attack* and a slower *Release*, like the configuration shown in Figure 6.29:

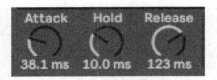

Figure 6.29: A longer Attack and slower Release on Ableton Live's Gate.

Then, if you add your distortion after this Gate, *only* sounds that breach the *Threshold* will be sounded (and therefore distorted). This can be seen in Figure 6.30:

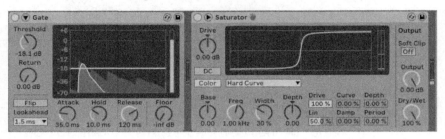

Figure 6.30: The signal chain to distort sounds above the Gate's Threshold.

Now, what if you wished to distort sounds *below* the *Threshold*, not above?

Like many gates, Ableton Live's Gate has a function called *Flip*, which reverses the operation of the Gate – with *Flip* activated, only sounds *below* the *Threshold* are allowed through. This is shown in Figure 6.31:

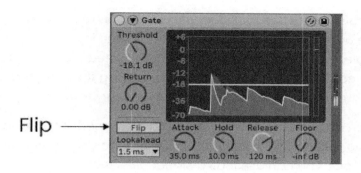

Flip ⟶

Figure 6.31: The Flip function in Ableton Live's Gate.

As you may have noticed, this setup allows for duplication of the original sound. For example, if your Gate is not in *Flip* mode, then the sounds above the *Threshold* will play beside your originals. This may not be desirable.

Should you wish to mitigate this impact, the answer is simple. Just as we've previously looked at, you can route your signal to a new audio track. On this audio track you place a Gate with an identical *Threshold* to the Gate on your auxiliary track – but using *Flip* to reverse the effect. When you do this, you may need to tighten your *Attack* and *Release Thresholds* to create a continuous sound. This is shown in Figure 6.32:

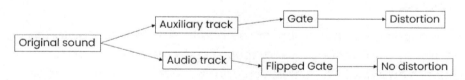

Figure 6.32: The signal chain to distort sounds above or below a certain amplitude threshold using a Gate.

One advantage of gated distortion is that you don't need to use the originating sound itself to trigger the Gate – you can use a

Sidechain input instead. *Sidechain* allows you to select an external source as a trigger for the Gate instead of the input. You could, for example, pass a whole track through the gated distortion and then create rhythmic automation by isolating those rhythmic elements you want to use as triggers for your Gate.

You can do this in Ableton by creating a separate drum track, one that you wish to use to trigger the Gate. Once you've created this drum track, you can use it as a *Sidechain* source within the Gate unit, as shown in Figure 6.33:

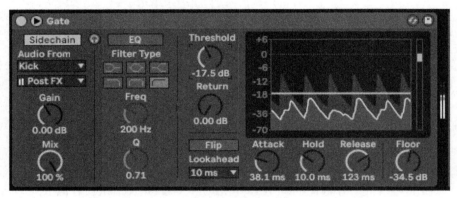

Figure 6.33: Using a Sidechain source within Ableton Live's Gate.

By doing this, you are automating exactly *when* this distortion is applied.

Equally, you can use a similar method to ensure that a distorted auxiliary track is suppressed according to the intensity of the incoming signal. To do this, you can use *Sidechain* compression.

Sidechain is where the compressor is triggered into action using an external signal, rather than the input signal – just like the *Sidechain* function on a Gate. This means that rather than calculating whether its usual input signal has met the *Threshold*, the compressor instead calculates whether the *Sidechain* signal has met the *Threshold*. This signal flow is illustrated in Figure 6.34:

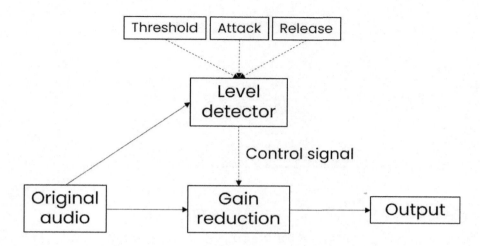

Figure 6.34: The signal flow for Sidechain compression.

Imagine an input signal 6dB above the *Threshold*, but a *Sidechain* input level only 3dB above the *Threshold*, as shown in Figure 6.35:

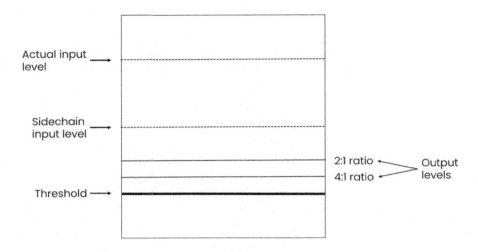

Figure 6.35: A diagram of a compressor using the Sidechain input level and the ratio to decide on an output level.

As you can see in Figure 6.35, even though the input level is 6dB above the *Threshold*, a 2:1 *Ratio* compresses the sound to 1.5dB over the *Threshold*. This is because the compressor is analysing the *Sidechain* input level of 3dB above the *Threshold*.

To provide an example, Figure 6.36 depicts the waveform of a pad with no compression applied:

Figure 6.36: The waveform of a pad with no compression applied, as depicted in Ableton Live.

Figure 6.37 depicts the waveform of a kick drum:

Figure 6.37: The waveform of a kick drum, as depicted in Ableton Live.

If the pad is routed to a compressor, however, and the kick drum is used as the *Sidechain* source, the 'bounce' of the kick drum makes an impression upon the pad levels, as seen in Figure 6.38:

Figure 6.38: The waveform of a compressed pad with a kick drum as its Sidechain source, as depicted in Ableton Live.

This can be further observed on the compressor's display, as shown in Figure 6.39:

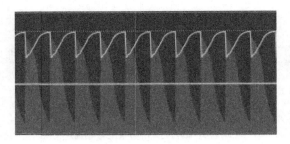

Figure 6.39: Ableton Live's Compressor's display, showing a kick drum being used as a Sidechain source.

Another interesting aspect of *Sidechain* is that it doesn't require the source to be audible on the main output. This means that a producer can *Sidechain* a rhythm source into a compressor to add a rhythmic bounce to a sound, even though that rhythm source can't be heard on the main output. Equally, the source can be made audible, so that the levels of a guitar drop slightly when a vocalist sings, for example.

On this basis, you can use *Sidechain* compression to balance the level of your distorted auxiliary track with the level of your output signal. For example, consider the guitar loop visualised in Ableton Live in Figure 6.40, with its peaks and troughs:

Figure 6.40: A guitar loop depicted in Ableton Live.

When playing the original and the distorted copy simultaneously, the peaks of the loop will also create peaks in the auxiliary track, thus overloading your overall mix, which can be a challenge.

However, you can use *Sidechain* compression within your auxiliary track so that the level of your distortion channel is suppressed in response to the peaks in the source material, as shown in Figure 6.41:

Figure 6.41: Sidechain compression on Ableton Live's Compressor.

To do this:

1. Add a compressor after your distortion within the auxiliary track's effects chain.
2. Activate *Sidechain* (or set your input source as *Sidechain* – depending on your compressor's layout) and set your *Sidechain* input to the source material.
3. Set the *Input Gain* so that the peaks reach around 0dB on your *Threshold* meter.
4. Set quite a high ratio (between 4:1 and 10:1), and bring your *Attack* down to around 1ms, and your *Release* up to 100ms, then work from there to find a sweet spot. Listen to how your signal's level is 'bouncing' in time to the *Sidechain* input. When you've found the sweet spot, it will seem to do so in a way that works rhythmically with the signal being compressed.
5. Move your *Threshold* down until you're happy with the result. The lower the *Threshold* goes; the more compression will be applied.

This method means that not only can you use distortion as part of an auxiliary effects chain, adding delay, reverb and other effects that you want – but you can automate the balancing of the levels between your auxiliary track and your main signal.

Now that we've looked at three different methods of parallel mixing, you may have noticed a pattern:

1. You need to create a distorted and an undistorted copy of your source sound.
2. You can send one copy to an additional audio track, and another copy to an auxiliary track for distortion.
3. You can split by frequency using an EQ, or by stereo state using a Utility plugin, or by audio level using a Gate.

Recommended Exercises

Consider the following questions:

1. Why is it important to ensure that the output level of your distorted track is the same as when distortion is bypassed/turned off?
2. What's the difference between harsh distortion with *Dry/Wet* set to a low value, and gentle distortion with *Wet* set to 100%?
3. What's the purpose of using EQ with distortion?
4. What are three methods of parallel processing, to split your sound by frequency, stereo space, and amplitude?

Chapter 7: Working with distortion

Now that you understand the varieties of distortion, and tips for using it in your work, we shall now explore the application of distortion in two contexts: its application to instruments, and its application within your mix.

Using Distortion on Instruments

Let's look at some broad tips to help you use distortion on specific instruments. As we've discussed, distortion is a matter of individual taste. However, many producers want to warm their tracks up in a simple, effective manner. This section will help you do this.

Drums

Drums can benefit a great deal from distortion. Tube and tape emulation can sound fantastic, imbuing your drums with punch, warmth, and depth.

When working with electronic drums, be careful with the lowest and highest frequencies. Excessive distortion can remove some of the power and punch of the kick, as well as detract from some of the sparkle of hi-hats, cymbals and tambourines.

An example is shown in Figure 7.1 below – notice how after distortion, this 909 kick drum has more presence in the 200-2kHz range. Whilst this hasn't reduced the amplitude of the area under 200Hz in absolute terms, it has reduced it relative to the 200-2kHz range. This has increased the overall amplitude of the kick and will force you to turn it down in the mix, reducing the kick drum's power.

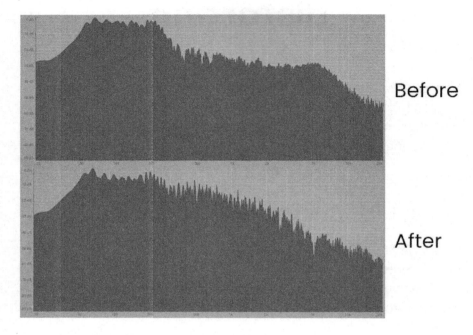

Before

After

Figure 7.1: A 909 kick drum before and after harsh distortion.

You may therefore wish to mitigate this impact by splitting your drums across different mixer channels, applying a low frequency algorithm (using the *Frequency* parameter) to low frequency sounds such as the kick and lower toms, and a high frequency algorithm to high frequency sounds such as hi-hats and cymbals.

Digital samples from drum kits such as the 808 and 909 can often sound flat compared to the drums you hear on commercial releases. This is because of a combination of factors, including high-end studios using hardware drum machines, producers adding some saturation to drums, and the saturation added during the mastering stage. This is particularly the case when your reference tracks are from the 1980s or 1990s. On this basis, a subtle amount of saturation can help give electronic drums the dynamism that hardware drum machines possess.

If you're using non-electronic drum samples, you may find that kicks, snares and toms are the best targets for distortion, as distorting these elements can create power, without detracting from the elegant timbre of the cymbals.

Don't forget that distortion can flatten the dynamic range of drums. Ensure that the dynamics of your drums still sound natural, particularly if you're using distortion together with compression.

You can consider using bitcrushing to create lo-fi drums, particularly on elements with substantial high frequency content. Be careful about using bitcrushing your kick, however, if you wish to maintain the kick's power.

Tape distortion can also be useful on synthwave drums, particularly drums generated by synthesized white noise.

To summarise:

1. Tube and tape emulation work well on drums, although bitcrushing can be useful to create lo-fi drums.
2. Watch out for the lowest and highest frequencies, which can be dampened by distortion. You may wish to put your low frequency drums on a different mixer channel to your high frequency drums to distort both separately.
3. Watch out for distortion flattening the dynamic range of the drums – make sure they still sound natural.
4. Electronic drum samples particularly benefit from some subtle warming up.

Bass

As the anchor that underpins your tracks, your bass can be a great target for distortion. Sub-basses below 80Hz that sound great on studio and club systems can often become lost on speakers with no sub-bass range, such as phones or small

Bluetooth speakers. This means that distorting basslines can give them presence in the frequency range that smaller speakers can reproduce.

Bass takes a huge amount of sonic space, so warmth in this area is important. However, keeping the fundamental frequency of the bassline is vital. Too much *Drive* emphasises the harmonics, meaning that the sheer power of the bass fundamental frequency is lost. Notice how in Figure 7.2 the amplitude of the lowest frequencies is lower at 100% *Drive*:

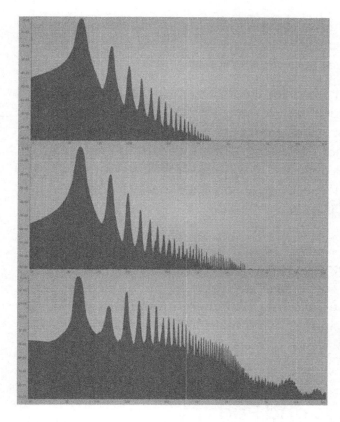

Figure 7.2: A comparison of 0% Drive, 50% Drive, and 100% Drive on a bass.

If you find that this happens when you distort a bass, try processing in parallel to mitigate the damage to the lower end of your bass, ensuring that the sub-bass remains undistorted.

Broadly, adding a small amount of analogue-emulating distortion can add a great deal of weight and warmth to your bass – just make sure the texture is consistent with your sound design. If a plugin gives your bass a warm, cosy feeling, it may not sit well in a cold track.

If you're working with genres where your bassline occupies a huge frequency range, such as EDM or drum and bass, you may consider creating three copies of your bass: a sub-bass that you leave alone, a middle section you distort slightly, and an upper end you add a great deal of distortion to.

Consider also the harmonics created by the oscillator you use. Don't forget that sawtooth waves create warm odd and even harmonics, square waves create cooler, odd harmonics, and sine waves create no harmonics at all. On that basis, square waves sound better when warmed up by tube-emulating distortion, whereas sawtooth waves can sound quite messy if additional harmonic content is added.

To summarise:

1. Adding distortion to basslines can give them presence, particularly on smaller speakers.
2. Keeping the bassline's fundamental frequency is vital.
3. Try processing in parallel if distortion causes damage to the lower end of your bass.

Synths, Leads and Pads

Distortion on synthesizers, leads and pads that occupy the centre of the frequency range can be tricky. These are sounds that are naturally harmonically rich, and distortion adds to these harmonics. Additionally, distortion can strip away the dynamic range of a sound.

Particularly when used on digital synthesizer plugins, some subtle tube saturation can sound fantastic. Remember, however, that this distortion can increase the perceived prominence of your instrument in the mix. For example, if you have a pad that sits in the background, distortion can draw attention to it – which draws attention away from the other elements of your mix.

An important concept to remember when distorting melodic chords is **intermodulation distortion**. This is where inharmonic frequencies are added to the signal by distortion. Intermodulation distortion can sound messy and unpleasant. It is caused by distortion adding additional harmonics to an already harmonically rich timbre, generating a huge number of harmonics, many of which lack a harmonic relationship to one another. You'll know you've encountered intermodulation distortion when a chord sounds good without distortion but sounds poor when distorted.

If you are aiming for a great deal of energy and dynamism in your track, pads are a great target for *Sidechain* distortion. You can also, on some instruments, control the amount of distortion at note level by mapping the note velocity to the distortion amount. An example of this in Lennar Digital's Sylenth1 is shown in Figure 7.3:

Figure 7.3: Routing Velocity control changes to Distortion Amount in Sylenth1.

Be careful, however, if your sound is one that possesses a great deal of high frequency 'sparkle'. Distortion can replace this 'sparkle' with a characteristic 'fuzz', which may not be the desired outcome if your instrument is meant to soar above the mix.

Melodic instruments in this frequency range such as leads, keys, or stabs can all be suitable targets for subtle bitcrushing if you wish to create a harsh, digital sound. Bitcrushing can also be used in place of a filter to 'close down' a sound in an arrangement.

To summarise:

1. Distorting synthesizers is great to add to the harmonics of a sound but be careful of stripping away the sound's dynamic range.
2. Tube saturation in particular sounds excellent on digital synthesizer plugins.
3. Watch out for intermodulation distortion, particularly on harmonically rich sounds such as pad chords.
4. Sidechain distortion can work well on pads.
5. Be careful when distorting sounds that possess high frequency 'sparkle', as distortion can dampen this.
6. Bitcrushing can be useful to create a harsh, digital sound, or to 'close down' a sound in an arrangement.

Vocals

Vocals are usually the most prominent part of a track, and therefore the most critical to get right. Consider tube saturation if you're looking to warm them up gently, but more harsh distortion such as bitcrushing if you're looking for an extreme effect, such as highly prominent ad-libs around the lead vocal.

Consider applying EQ after the saturation to control the most prominent harmonics, as well as a de-essing compressor if the saturation has made 's' sounds too prominent.

A starting point for de-essing is a compressor focussed only on the 's' frequencies – normally around 3-10kHz. An example in Ableton Live is shown in Figure 7.4:

Figure 7.4: A de-essing compressor in Ableton Live.

This is useful if you want the warmth of distortion without the high frequency harshness that it can sometimes create.

Additionally, you can process vocals in parallel, for example by adding distortion to a copy of the vocal, or to the vocal's reverberation. This can subtly warm up the vocal without detracting too much from the singer's voice.

The most important thing to remember is that a little distortion goes a long way. We're used to human voices sounding delicate, and distorting vocals violates that expectation. Use that information how you will!

To summarise:

1. Vocals are the most critical part of a track and require careful consideration.

2. Tube saturation can warm up vocals gently, while bitcrushing can create harsh, cold effects.

3. EQ can be applied after saturation to control prominent harmonics, and a de-essing compressor can control prominent sibilance.

4. Processing in parallel can add warmth without detracting from the singer's voice.

5. Use distortion sparingly; vocals are expected to sound delicate!

Mixing with Distortion

Distorting individual elements of your tracks can bring its own set of challenges in mixing down your work. If you're not used to mixing distorted tracks, you may find that your work sounds flat, or unbalanced, or that your distorted layers can drown out your undistorted layers. Therefore, here are some tips for mixing with distortion:

1. Pieces of recorded music that sound highly distorted have some undistorted elements. This creates a balanced mix, reduces listener fatigue, and contrasts the distorted elements with the undistorted ones. For example, listen to *Raw Power (Iggy Pop Mix)* by The Stooges. Even though the guitar and vocals, at the front and centre of the mix, are extremely distorted, the drums, tambourine and piano are clean, thus creating a counterbalance to the distorted elements. If you wish to make every element of your mix sound distorted, try to ensure that at least *some* elements are less distorted, otherwise your listener won't have a point of reference.

2. We've discussed the use of EQ when distorting vocals but remember that *any* distorted element can generate a lot of high harmonics. When distorting several elements, select the ones that should have that distortive crackle, and cut the high frequencies of the ones that shouldn't using EQ. This should keep the distortive crackle nicely emphasised within the mix.

3. Be careful of elements with stray high frequencies that can also interfere with your distortion. Examples include long reverb or delay tails.

4. If you are distorting a track with a lot of bass, for example an 808 kick, distortion will add harmonics. The added harmonics may bring your bass elements into conflict with the lower end of your mid-range instruments. Examples include synthesizer stabs, vocals, or even the fundamental frequency of a snare drum. Too much content in the 200–500Hz frequency range can create a muddy-sounding mix. Therefore, be judicious in this range, and decide whether your distorted bass element of the lower end of your instruments should take precedence.

To summarise this section, Figure 7.5 is an example of the basic signal flow of a mix that uses distortion:

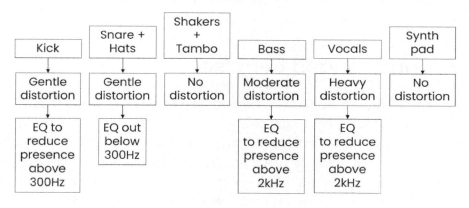

Figure 7.5: A basic signal flow of a mix that uses distortion.

As you can see, the heaviest distortion is on the bass and the vocals. This places additional emphasis on these elements. To compensate, the drum kit has gentle distortion. The shakers, tambourine, and synth pad – the most delicate elements – receive no distortion. This balances the distorted elements.

Meanwhile, EQ is used to keep the frequency content of the distorted elements in check. The kick has its presence above 300Hz reduced to make way for the snare channel. The bass and vocals have their presence above 2kHz reduced to make way for the shakers, tambourine, and pad.

To summarise:

1. Distortion creates mixing challenges, such as flat layers, or distorted layers overpowering undistorted ones. Try keeping some layers undistorted to keep the mix balanced.
2. Use EQ to control high harmonics and stray high frequencies.
3. Be careful of muddiness in the bass range.

In the next chapter, we'll look at the application of distortion principles within real-world music production situations.

Recommended Exercises

1. Create an element in the middling frequency range (such as a lead, pad, or guitar).
   a. Add a substantial amount of distortion to this track. If possible, use a plugin with *Output* volume control.
   b. Using the mixer, compare the level of the signal with the distortion on to the level of the signal with the distortion off (i.e., bypassed).
   c. Try to match the level of the distorted signal with the level of the bypassed signal.
   d. Now that both signals are at the same level, consider whether your perception of the distortion has changed.

2. Remove the distortion you've added to this element. Then, use an auxiliary track for some parallel distortion on this element. Try:
    a. Splitting your track by frequency range.
    b. Splitting your track by stereo width.
    c. Splitting your track by dynamics, using a Gate or compressor.

3. If you have a track that you've already written saved to your computer, save a copy of its file. Using this copy, create a 'hot' mix of your track, where at least two elements have a great deal of distortion on them. Don't worry, you don't have to share this with anyone! Use this as an opportunity to practice the instrument distortion and mixing tips in this chapter.

Chapter 8: Distortion in action

Now that you understand the theory of distortion and you've practiced it using the exercises in this book, here are five real-life examples of using distortion in a music production context. You can hear audio examples at **https://distortion.producers.guide**

Example One: Giving a Bass some Edge

In this first example, we'll look at a routine use of distortion – warming up a bassline.

Sometimes, you may find that though a bassline's bottom end has depth, it lacks the presence that good basslines have. Therefore, you may wish to warm it up using some distortion. Here is an example of my own.

The first step was to add some *Filter Drive* to the synthesizer itself. The result of this is shown in Figure 8.1:

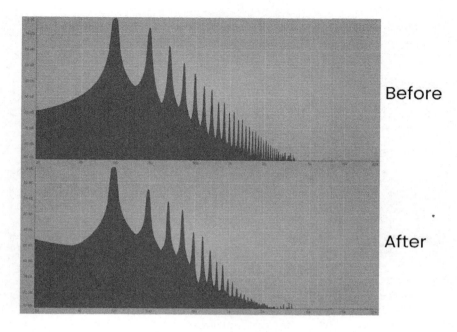

Figure 8.1: The effect of Filter Drive on a bassline.

As you can see, this added some harmonic presence around the 160-400Hz mark, as well as a small amount of top end resonance above 2kHz. This increased the feeling of warmth.

I felt it could do with further warmth, so I added an analogue saturation plugin.

My first step was to use the *Trim* function to control the level coming into the plugin, as it works optimally when the level of the incoming sound hovers around the 0dB mark.

I then turned *Drive* up to its highest level to hear the effects of the algorithm, then dialled *Drive* back down until the bass sounded warm, but not harsh.

Then, because this was a bass, I moved *Frequency* to LF to focus the saturation on lower frequencies.

Finally, to ensure that I was hearing the effects of the saturation itself (and not just an increase in the sound's level), I enabled and bypassed the plugin, comparing the levels between the two. The saturated sound was louder, so I brought the plugin's *Output* down to where the meter neared 0, showing that the audio coming in and the audio going out were at about the same level.

Finally, I wanted to highlight the harmonics that I had added to the sound, so I used an EQ to increase the amplitude of these harmonics, as shown in Figure 8.2:

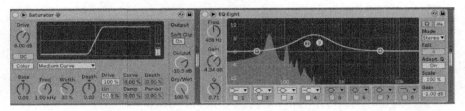

Figure 8.2: Highlighting harmonics using EQ in Ableton Live.

This led to a warmer, more enveloping sound, as seen in the 200–400Hz area of Figure 8.3:

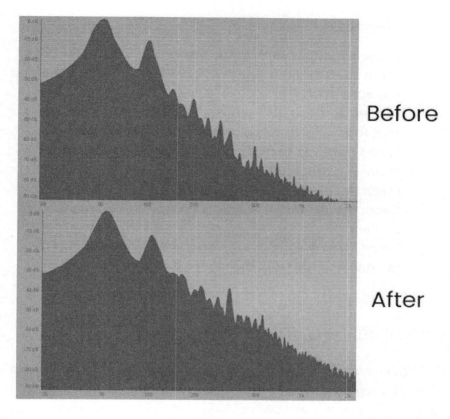

Figure 8.3: *This highlighting of harmonics led to more presence in the 200-400Hz region.*

There's an interesting question to be asked – why did I use distortion, when I could have increased the *Cutoff* of the low-pass filter on my synthesizer?

The reason is that my bassline was a combination of two oscillators: a sine wave to create power, and a square wave to create subtle harmonic presence. These two oscillators create a great deal of bass power together, but they have little in the way of even harmonics – the harmonics that impart warmth upon a sound. Therefore, analogue-simulating saturation, enhanced slightly with EQ, did a great job of warming this bass up and providing it with some presence.

So, let's summarise this process:

1. I added some warmth at the filter stage using *Filter Drive*. This was so that the sound was already warm as it entered any saturation.
2. I added an analogue-emulating saturation plugin, using *Trim* to ensure its output amplitude matched the input. This use of *Trim* was so that my judgement wasn't clouded by a change in amplitude.
3. I selected the correct amount of *Drive* and selected a low frequency algorithm in order to preserve low frequency content.
4. I used EQ to emphasise the harmonics that distortion enhanced, in order to highlight these to the listener.

Example Two: Improving an 808

The 808 is a classic drum machine used in many genres of music, especially hip-hop and electro. As we've discussed, the digital samples that come with DAW software often lack the grit and warmth of real hardware, particularly after that hardware has been mixed and mastered in analogue gear. On that basis, warming up an 808 drum track when working digitally will often be helpful.

Luckily, in terms of music production, there are only two elements of an 808 drum beat we need to think about in terms of distortion if our goal is to warm up the whole beat:

a. The kick drum, and
b. Everything else.

This is because we want the sub-bass power of the kick to maintained.

To split these, therefore, I didn't need to do anything technically impressive – I simply programmed the kick drum onto one MIDI channel, and everything else onto another MIDI channel. I used several MIDI channels for the non-kick percussion, so I grouped them onto a bus track.

Let's have a look at how I treated the kick drum first.

As you can see in Figure 8.4, an 808 kick has two elements that make it sound good:

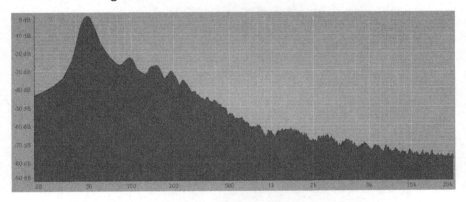

Figure 8.4: A spectrum analysis of an 808 kick drum.

    a.   A chunky sub-bass under 90Hz
    b.   Harmonics that add presence and warmth above 90Hz

Because of this, I used parallel mixing to process the two frequency ranges separately.

First, the sub-bass could be left alone, as I did not wish to add extra harmonics that may conflict with the harmonics already present. I then needed to add saturation to the content above 90Hz.

This could be accomplished using the technique we discussed in Chapter 6. I therefore:

    1.   Created an audio track followed by an auxiliary track.
    2.   Routed the kick's output to the audio track.

3. I used the auxiliary *Send* to create a duplicate copy of the kick.

Once I'd done that, I could use an EQ to filter the audio track's frequencies to those below 90Hz only. Then, I could use an EQ to filter the auxiliary track's frequencies to those above 90Hz. This process effectively splits the two tracks by frequency. This is shown in Figure 8.5:

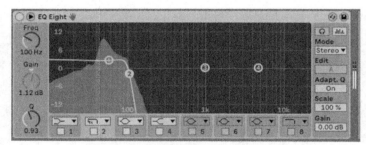

Audio track

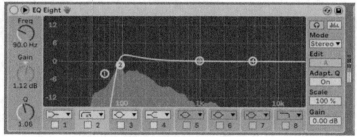

Auxiliary channel

Figure 8.5: Splitting the signal into an audio track and an auxiliary track using Ableton Live's EQ Eight.

The auxiliary track (the content of the kick above 90Hz) could then be warmed up with analogue-emulating saturation. Here, I used an algorithm that emphasised the low frequencies, in order to preserve their warmth.

When comparing the kick (combining both sides of the frequency split) before and after saturation, we can see that even though some of the top end click is lost, there's much more warmth and presence added to the 100-600Hz range – and this is the range that matters when creating an enveloping lower end. Before and after this saturation is compared in Figure 8.6:

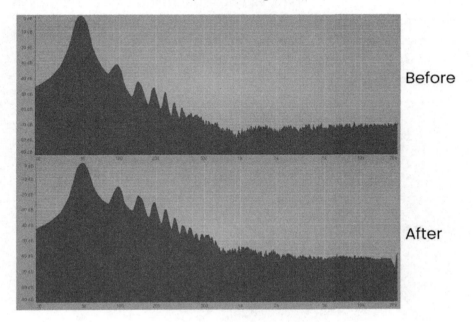

Figure 8.6: Warmth and presence has been added to the 100Hz-600Hz range of the kick drum.

The next step was to saturate the higher end, i.e., the instruments above the kick. This was easy to do – a vintage-emulating saturator with gentle *Drive* should accomplish this.

First, I used the *Trim* function to boost the level of the incoming signal to peak around 0dB.

I then opted for a *Drive* of around halfway and brought the *Output* down to ensure that I could listen to the effect that the plugin was having without creating additional distortion because of an excessively high output level entering the mixer.

I used a neutral algorithm to derive a chunky, compressed, bright sound. Once I was happy with the character, I experimented with *Drive* to find the right amount of distortion. I found that a small to moderate amount provided the sweet spot between character and clarity.

As you can see, compared to some experiments we've undertaken so far in this book, the difference in the frequency response is minimal. This isn't an issue, because all we're looking to do is warm up the top end slightly – not transform it. This difference is visualised in Figure 8.7:

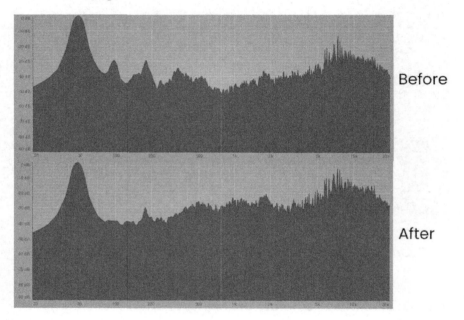

Figure 8.7: The entire drum beat before and after saturation.

As you can see, the main difference is that a lot of warmth has been added around 500-1,500Hz, likely harmonics from the snare drum. There's also some sparkle added between 2kHz and 5kHz.

Overall, these simple steps have transformed this 808 beat from something bland to something with the grit, sparkle and interest –

something far more suited to a professional level of music production.

Let's summarise the steps taken:

1. I moved the kick and the other percussion to two separate MIDI channels, so that I could apply distortion to the kick alone.
2. I split the kick at 90Hz, to distort the harmonics above 90Hz, but leave the sub-bass under 90Hz unchanged. This is because distorting the area under 90Hz wouldn't add any value, whereas the presence of the kick could be enhanced by increasing the harmonic interest above 90Hz.
3. I added analogue-emulating distortion to the kick, above 90Hz only. I chose analogue-emulating distortion due to the addition of warm even harmonics.
4. I added analogue-emulating distortion to the second MIDI channel, the one containing drums other than the kick. This was so that I could apply a low frequency emphasising algorithm to the kick above 90Hz, without having to apply the same algorithm to the other drums.

Example Three: Evoking Nostalgia

In this example, I had a nostalgic synthwave chord sequence.

I wanted to give the synthesized bassline warmth, presence, and a vintage feel. On this basis, I opted for a type of saturation that was naturally prevalent in the 1980s: tape saturation.

Being vintage tape saturation, the more saturation is added, the more the top end is dampened. This would be fine on a single layer, but in this mix, I wanted a top end presence. Therefore, I found the best compromise between a top end presence and warmth to be around +8dB of *Drive*.

The next step was to add some vintage tape hiss using a *Noise* parameter. The right amount was enough that it wasn't clearly audible, but you'd miss it if it wasn't there.

Then, it was time to add the vintage tape effects: *Wow* and *Flutter*. The *Wow* was pleasing to listen to, a slowly oscillating harmonic destabilisation. The *Flutter*, not so much – a harsh LFO. However, both had their place.

For the *Wow* parameter, I wanted another compromise – enough detuning to create a nostalgic sense, but not enough to be noticeable by the listener, as this would sound cheesy. I found a small amount to be right.

Given that *Flutter* is more destructive, only a miniscule amount was required to create a gentle sense of nostalgia. Finally, I assessed the level of the saturated track with the plugin switched on and then bypassed, and I found the plugin lowered the peak level of the track by 4.2dB. I therefore set the *Output* level to +4.2dB. This is so that I could assess the effect of the plugin rationally without my judgement being clouded by additional loudness.

With this saturation applied; the sound was warmer, bigger, and more nostalgic. This was especially pronounced in the 1kHz–5kHz range, as shown Figure 8.8:

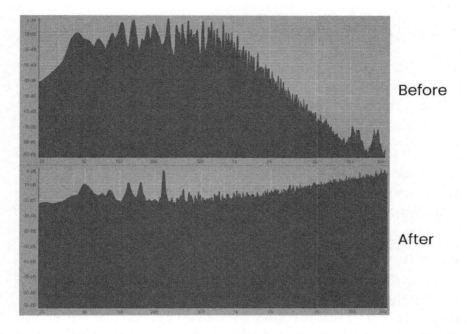

Before

After

Figure 8.8: Spectrum analysis before and after tape distortion.

Let's summarise the steps taken:

1. I added tape saturation with a significant amount of *Drive* to give the bass warmth, presence, and a vintage feel.
2. I added tape noise to enhance the vintage feel.
3. I used *Wow* and *Flutter* to create some subtle inharmonic oscillations to further recreate the 1980s atmosphere.
4. I reduced the *Output* level to match the input level of the saturation to ensure that I was evaluating the saturation fairly – and that my judgement wasn't clouded by the track simply being louder!

In the next example, we'll look at saturating some stereo delays, bringing them to the listener's attention.

Example Four: Saturated Delays

In this example, we'll look at delays used in ambient Dub Techno chords. Usually, stereo delay is used to add some subtle, rhythmic space – but what if you wished to draw the listener's attention to these delays?

You could, of course, simply increase the volume of these delays, but in addition, some presence and character can make them stand out more in the mix. In this section, we will explore adding this presence and character.

Being an intricate piece of Dub Techno, the two synthesized chord layers in this example already have some reverb, distortion and delay added – but I had added a further delay to an auxiliary track. Note that being an auxiliary track, I didn't want to create a duplicate of my original sound, so I placed the *Dry/Wet* parameter of the delay at 100% so that only the delays are heard through the auxiliary track, not the original signal. This is shown in Figure 8.9:

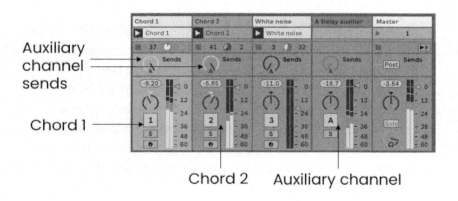

Figure 8.9: The signal flow used to create saturated delays.

After this delay, I didn't want lower frequencies causing conflict with any other elements. I added an EQ to keep this auxiliary track delay nice and clean. This can be seen in Figure 8.10:

Figure 8.10: Setting the Dry/Wet to 100% means only the delays are routed to the auxiliary track.

With these in place, the next step was to consider how to bring these delays to the listener's attention.

Because the goal was to for the distortion to be attention-grabbing (as opposed to warming a sound up), I could look at more harsh forms of distortion, with an emphasis on odd harmonics. Here, I chose a waveshaping saturator. I used a tough waveshaping curve, as shown in Figure 8.11, with a +12dB *Drive*.

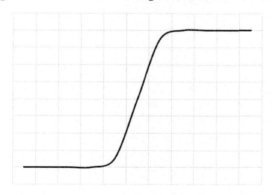

Figure 8.11: A harsh waveshaping curve.

Ordinarily, this would be too harsh for most instruments, but this added a lot of brightness and presence to the delays.

This level of distortion, however, amplified the signal far too much, and I therefore brought the *Output* level down by 20dB to compensate for the excessive audio level this had created.

The distortion sounded good, but it needed further grit, harshness, and hiss to make it stand out. Simple harmonic distortion wouldn't be enough for that, so I chose a bitcrusher.

First, I set the *Dry/Wet* to 100% *Wet* so that I could hear the full effect of the bitcrusher.

Then, I experimented with the *Bit Depth* and *Sample Rate* to give me the sound I desired. This was difficult: I wanted the destructive sound of the bitcrusher, but I wanted the result to bear some harmonic relation to the chords themselves.

I therefore settled upon a *Downsample* of 6 and a *Sample Rate* of /2.

When comparing the delays that went into the Saturator and Bitcrusher with the delays that came out, there's some notable differences, as seen Figure 8.12:

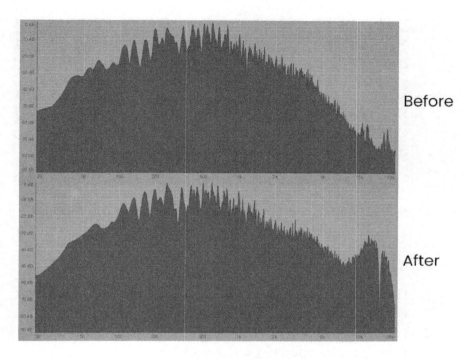

Before

After

Figure 8.12: A comparison of the spectrum analysis of the delays before and after the use of TAL-Bitcrusher.

What was a delay sequence that peaked around 1–3kHz now peaked above 5kHz, with the high frequency content drawing the listener's attention.

I felt, however, that this degree of very high frequency content may interfere with other high frequency elements. I therefore added a filter (using an EQ) to bring these highest frequencies under control, as shown in Figure 8.13:

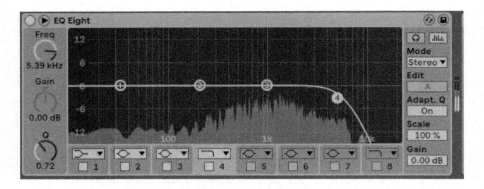

Figure 8.13: An EQ used in Ableton Live to bring the highest frequencies of a delay under control.

Let's summarise the steps taken in this example:

1. I added a Delay plugin to an auxiliary track, set to 100% *Wet*.
2. I used *Send* to drive both chords to the auxiliary track.
3. I added an EQ after the Delay on the auxiliary channel to filter out unneeded lower frequencies.
4. I added harsh waveshaping distortion to the auxiliary channel to give the auxiliary channel a substantial amount of 'crunch'.
5. I reduced the *Output* level of the waveshaper to -20dB to compensate for the high amount of output amplitude that the harsh waveshaper had generated.
6. I added some subtle bitcrushing to give the auxiliary channel even more of an edge through its high frequency distortion.

In the next and final example, let's have a look at creating a warm, distortive environment around a vocal recording.

Example Five: Warming Up a Vocal

For this example, I sought to warm up a vocal sample. The sample I used was a clean recording of someone singing a scale.

I didn't wish, however, for the vocal sample itself to be distorted – I wanted warmth and distortion in the 'atmosphere' surrounding the vocal. On that basis, I distorted an auxiliary track with reverb placed upon it. Let's explore how I went about that task.

First, just like with the distorted delays, I 'sent' the vocal to an auxiliary track, as seen in Figure 8.14:

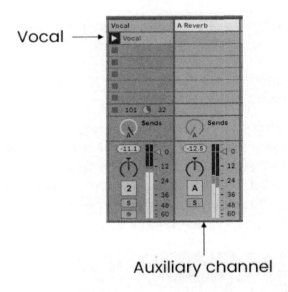

Figure 8.14: A vocal being 'sent' to an auxiliary track in Ableton Live.

I then placed my Reverb upon this auxiliary track, as shown in Figure 8.15:

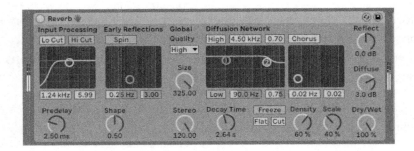

Figure 8.15: The Reverb added in Ableton Live to the vocal's auxiliary track.

This reverberated vocal needed warming up, so I opted for analogue-emulating saturation.

Being a vocal, I chose a high frequency response algorithm. I then drove the plugin harshly using 7dB of *Drive*. This created a beautifully warm, enveloping sound. The only issue was that this created a conflict. The start of the vocal phrase created a reverberation. This reverberation conflicted with the end of the vocal phrase, as visualised in Figure 8.16:

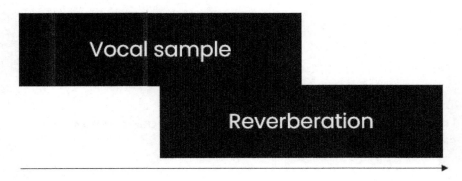

Figure 8.16: The conflict between the vocal sample and its reverberation.

Therefore, I needed a method to prevent the vocal sample overlapping with its distorted reverberation.

I added *Sidechain* compression to the auxiliary track, using the original vocal as an input. This meant that the vocal forced the distorted reverb to 'duck', keeping it away from the vocal itself. The compression configuration is shown Figure 8.17:

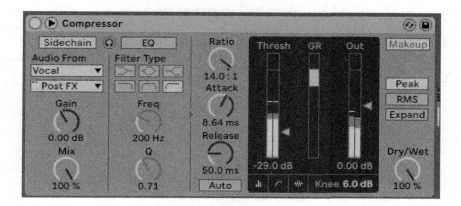

Figure 8.17: Sidechain compression added to the auxiliary track in Ableton Live.

Finally, when comparing the frequency analysis before and after the distortion, I could see that the effects chain had created an unpleasant low frequency rumble, as well as an overemphasis around 800Hz. I therefore used EQ to remove this rumble, and the overemphasised harmonic, to ensure that this vocal could sit correctly in a mix. This is shown in Figure 8.18:

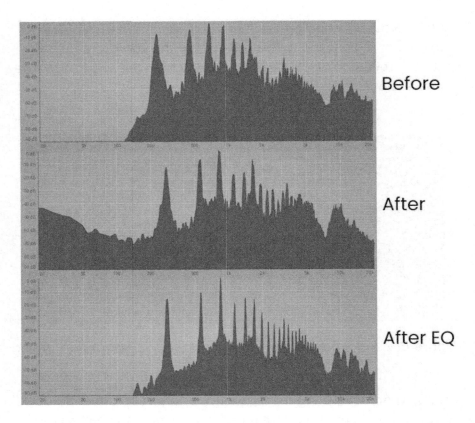

Figure 8.18: A comparison (from Ableton Live's EQ Eight) between the original vocal, the saturated version, and the version after EQ.

With that, the process of vocal saturation was complete.

Let's summarise the steps taken:

1. I created an auxiliary track and sent the vocals to this auxiliary track using *Send*. This was so that I could distort a separate copy of the vocal.
2. I added a reverb to this auxiliary track, setting it to 100% *Wet* to prevent duplication.
3. I added analogue-emulating saturation with +7dB of *Drive* to create quite harsh distortion.

4. I added *Sidechain* compression to the auxiliary track's effects chain, using the original vocal as a *Sidechain* source, so that the original vocal forced the auxiliary track to 'duck' in amplitude.
5. I added EQ to the auxiliary track to remove content under 800Hz, thus removing unneeded low frequency content from the auxiliary channel. This low frequency content added nothing to the overall sound and would've caused mixing issues.

These five examples conclude our exploration of distortion in action, but this is only the start of your journey in distortion. Before I leave you to begin this journey, there are three exercises below that I recommend you do.

Recommended Exercises

1. Load a drum track into your DAW, either by creating one or by using one you've written previously. Warm this drum track up using analogue-emulating distortion.

2. Load a lead into your DAW, either by creating one or by using one you've written previously. Experiment with warming this lead up, by comparing the results of analogue-emulating distortion, waveshaping distortion, and bitcrushing distortion.

3. Load a vocal into your DAW, either by creating one, acquiring one legally from a licensed sample pack, or by loading one you've used previously. Experiment with warming this lead up, by comparing the results of analogue-emulating distortion, waveshaping distortion, and bitcrushing distortion. Then, [6]send this vocal to an auxiliary channel, add a reverb or delay to this auxiliary channel, and experiment with distorting the reverb or delay.

Chapter 9: Conclusion

I hope this book has given you a thorough primer on the use of distortion in music production. We've reached the end of our journey exploring the myriad of ways in which you can use distortion to add character, depth, and emotion to your music.

Whilst this has presented a few different scenarios under which you might wish to harness the power of distortion in your work, your prospects are truly limitless. There are infinite combinations of different distortion types and degrees of distortion that can give your music that cutting edge. However, the fundamentals that I've provided you with in this book will enable you to use distortion with intelligence and intention.

We, as humans, don't like our art clean, ordered and precise. We need grit, we need chaos, and we need imperfections. It is these imperfections that we have the power to create and enhance using the power of distortion. Get it right and you can take your music, and your listeners, to new dimensions.

Glossary

Algorithm (distortion): Some distortion devices offer a variety of algorithms. Each algorithm is a unique distortion character.

Asymmetrical clipping: Clipping distortion where the bias point is off-centre.

Attack (Gate): The speed at which a Gate applies once the Threshold is met.

Auxiliary (aux) track: A mixer track you can pass audio to, but you can't record any audio or MIDI to it. It is often used by producers looking to apply the same effect to multiple mixer channels.

Bias (amplifier): The moving of the bias point within an amplifier to change the character of the distortion generated.

Bias (tape): An ultrasonic signal introduced into a tape recording to help maximise its fidelity, particularly higher frequencies.

Bias point: The crossover point (i.e., the centre point) of a waveform.

Bit: A unit of computer storage, set to 0 or 1.

Bit depth: The number of bits of information in each sample of audio.

Bitcrushing: Distortion created by reducing the bit depth of a sound. Can also be an umbrella term for any effect that reduces the bit depth of sample rate of a sound.

Bypass: Bypass prevents an effects unit from having an effect on a signal.

Crackle (vinyl): A distinctive 'crackle' sound when playing vinyl, caused by particles of dust within a vinyl record's grooves.

Distortion: The alteration of an information-bearing signal. In music, the signal is a sound wave. Can also suggest the application of harsh distortion within a musical piece (see Saturation and Overdrive)

Downsampling: To intentionally reduce the sample rate of a piece of audio.

Drive: Increasing the input amplitude of a signal into a processor (especially a filter or distortion plugin) in order to increase distortion.

Dry/Wet: A parameter that blends the unprocessed signal (the Dry signal) with the processed signal (The Wet signal).

Dynamic range: The difference between the quietest and the loudest part of a piece of audio.

Filter: An effect that allows you to choose which frequencies are allowed through the filter.

Filter (band-pass): A low-pass filter only allows signals around the selected frequency through.

Filter (high-pass): A low-pass filter only allows signals above the selected frequency through.

Filter (low-pass): A low-pass filter only allows signals below the selected frequency through.

Flanger: An audio effect created by mixing a signal with a slightly delayed copy of itself. It creates a shimmering, resonant effect.

Flip (Gate): With Flip activated, the operation of the Gate is reversed - only sounds below the Threshold are allowed through.

Floor (Gate): Floor defines the baseline amount of audio that the Gate passes when it is not active.

Flutter: Subtle frequency changes caused by the tape's movements as it moves across the playback head.

Frequency (distortion plugin parameter): A way of emphasising or keeping a particular portion of the frequency range, to mitigate against the adverse effect that distortion has on low and high frequencies.

Fundamental frequency: The lowest frequency of a waveform. In music, the fundamental frequency is usually the frequency of the note that the musician played.

Harmonic series: The sequence of tones whose frequency is a multiple of the fundamental frequency.

Harmonics: Also known as overtones. When an instrument is played, it not only produces the fundamental frequency, but a series of higher frequencies that are multiples of the fundamental. The balance of these overtones defines the timbre.

Hold (Gate): Hold defines how long the Gate continues after the sound dips back below the Threshold.

Input level/gain: A way of increasing or decreasing the amplitude of an input signal to optimise its amplitude as it enters a device.

Intermodulation distortion: Inharmonic frequencies added to the signal by distortion.

IPS: The speed at which tape crosses the heads, measured in Inches Per Second.

LFO: Low Frequency Oscillator. A rhythmic pulse used to modulate a parameter.

Meter: A device that displays the amplitude of a signal.

Missing fundamental: When a sound's overtones suggest a fundamental frequency, but that fundamental frequency is in fact not present. Even when the fundamental frequency is missing, the brain still perceives it as being there.

Mono: A signal with no stereo information.

Needle (vinyl): The part of a vinyl record player that picks up the waveform from the grooves on the record.

Noise (tape): See tape hiss.

Output level/gain: A parameter that allows you to increase or decrease the amplitude of the signal as it leaves the effects device.

Overdrive: Overdrive tends to mean fairly substantial distortion, but less than would be termed 'Distortion'.

Oversampling: Oversampling increases the sample rate beyond the normal sample rate in order to improve the quality and accuracy of an effect. This comes at a cost of increased processor load.

Overtones: See harmonics.

Release (Gate): The speed at which a Gate ceases to apply once the Threshold is no longer met.

Return (Gate): Return sets the difference between the level at which the Gate is activated and the level at which it is deactivated. This is useful when the Gate causes 'chattering' by opening and closing too rapidly.

Sample rate: The number of samples (i.e., snapshots) of audio taken per second.

Saturation: Saturation tends to mean gentle distortion, implying a slight warming up of a sound.

Send: A control that allows you to pass a chosen amount of the audio signal to an aux track.

Shape (waveshaper): A parameter that allows you to select or define the shape of the transfer function applied within a waveshaper.

Sidechain: The use of an external signal to trigger an effects device such as a compressor or Gate.

Speed (tape): The speed at which the tape crosses the heads, measured in IPS.

Stylus: The part of a vinyl record player that contains the needle.

Symmetrical clipping: Clipping distortion where the bias point is central.

Tape hiss: A background 'hiss' present on tape, caused by the size of the magnetic particles used to make the tape. Smaller particles generate less hiss.

Threshold (Gate): The level at which a Gate will allow audio through.

Tonearm: The movable part of a vinyl record player that permits the needle to follow the groove.

Transfer function: A mathematical way of mapping the relationship between the input and the output.

Trim: See Input level.

Waveshaping: An umbrella term for several techniques where the waveform of the sound undergoes a transformation of its timbre or dynamics, but with no significant changes to the frequency.

Wow: Subtle frequency modulation caused by slight changes in the speed of the tape motors.

Printed in Great Britain
by Amazon

31869453R00089